Celebrating Your Place at Our Table

Celebrating
Your Place at
Our Table

LAWRENCE C. C. CHU

Van Lachlan
Press

Credits

For Maggie—
We think of you often
and miss you deeply

VanLachlan Press
1000 Acacia Avenue
Los Altos, California 94022

ISBN 978-0-615-33367-0

To order additional copies:
Chef Chu's
1067 North San Antonio Road
Los Altos, California 94022
650.948.2696

Printed by
Phoenix Enterprise Group,
South San Francisco, California

PRINTED IN CHINA

Project Manager
Arlene McKellar

Art Director
Andrew Danish

Copy Chief
Nora Sweeny

Production
Amy Pilkington

Principal Photographer
Lori Eanes

Contributing Photographers
Nikolay Zurek
Mark Tuschman
Rick Smolan

Food Stylists
Pouké Halpern
Randy Mon

Illustrator
Cyndie Clark-Huegel

Props
Belinda Chung, B. K. Collections,
Los Altos, California

Gastronome/Instigator/Seer
Della van Heyst

Acknowledgments

I fervently believe the proverb

"Success has many parents,"

so I am grateful for the lifelong friendship of Martin and Sue Yan; the mentors and colleagues who opened the doors to the culinary world for me: Chris Yeo, John Hung Le, John Sikhattana, Joyce Jue, and fellow Asian Chefs Association founders and my close personal friends Khai and Mimi Duong; and for the countless others who have given graciously of their creative spark.

I am indebted to my inner circle of advisors who shared with me their gastronomic secrets and their love of glorious cooking: my father and chief inspiration H. T. Chu, professor and advisor Alec Cline, master chef Chen Shiang Shen, and brothers Jen Mei (James) and Frank Liou, who have served as my gifted executive chefs and close associates for many years.

This 40th Anniversary Celebration volume is the result of the dedicated work of a team of professionals. The most crucial "ingredients" to its production were Andrew Danish, whose aesthetic sense is inspirational and who gently kept us all on track; Arlene McKellar, whose dedication to transmit the authentic techniques and traditions of Asian cooking served as the essential foundation to this book; and Della van Heyst, my friend and trusted advisor for 40 years.

Finally, at the heart of it all, *Chef Chu's* is truly a family affair. My passion for this work and all the successes we've enjoyed over four decades would not be possible without the unflagging love, support and wise counsel of my wife, Ruth, whom I cherish and who is my source of strength and perseverance; the daily happy collaborations with Larry Jr. and Jennifer; and the loving and enthusiastic support of Christina, Howard, Jonathan, and my extended family, whose devotion to me makes my devotion to Chinese cooking possible.

—*Lawrence C. C. Chu*

THE CHU FAMILY
Top row: Jess Cruz, Howard Chu, Lawrence Chu Jr., Chef Lawrence Chu, Jon M. Chu. Seated: Jennifer Chu Cruz, Ruth Chu, Jolie Cruz, Jess Braden Cruz, Susanna Kwan Chu, Christina Chu

Thank you, dear patrons, for forty wonderful years.

In 1970, when Ruth and I opened the doors to a very modest restaurant, which we proudly called *Chef Chu's*—we were so excited. We wanted our guests to feel at home in our dining room, we wanted to share the delicacies we loved ourselves, and we passionately wanted to please the most discriminating palates. Diners arrived, and when satisfied smiles could be seen everywhere in our small dining area, I discovered that special joy that comes from the bond formed between diner and chef.

I have been wok-searing meats, steaming *bao*, and water-blanching almost everything green, and tossing spices every day for four decades—and the thrill of following an aromatic, beautiful serving as it is delivered to a table and then watching the reaction of happy people is a daily reward. Thank you for this pleasure.

There is a unique partnership that is formed between diners and chefs. From the very first days, you have been helping me identify the flavors that appeal to you most. With this understanding, I drill into my line chefs that consistency of taste is essential, so the tenth time you eat my *kung pao* chicken it tastes like the first. Knowing your tastes, then travelling extensively in China to rediscover exotic traditional ways of achieving a crunch, an aroma, a tenderness—I have been able to create new dishes you love to eat: *yee-mein*, pepper steak and now Gung Gung's oxtail stew named after my father-in-law Ben, host and greeter for many decades.

We have another passion in common: Family is important to you and it is a mainstay in my life. Thank you for letting us help you celebrate your most important occasions—birthdays, anniversaries, engagements, graduations—and all those many times in between when you just wanted to sit back, relax, and satisfy your hunger for something delicious.

Food connects, food is therapy, great food brings joy. We know these are your expectations when you come to *Chef Chu's*—beginning with the happy greeting when you come through our door. For forty years, a member of my family has always been on hand to welcome you with warmth. In the first decade, my wife Ruth met you while I cooked. Then her parents, Maggie and Ben, joined us as we grew. Now our children Larry and Jennifer are as familiar to regulars as you are to them. Christina helps out when she can. You'll see Howard, who is our food critic. And Jonathan, who comes up from Hollywood when his cravings for "home cooking" just have to be satisfied. The dining room at *Chef Chu's* often becomes our family's dining room, too. And through almost all of our forty years it's Charlie Ong whose familiar voice takes your reservation and also makes you feel at home. And while I mention them last, they are first at your table: our wonderful wait staff who are proud to have you in our dining room. We all look at every day as grand opening day.

So when I say "we," I speak for all of us. Thank you for being our extended family.

You will always have a place at our table.

—Chef Lawrence C. C. Chu

Contents

An Entrepreneur Among Entrepreneurs

For three decades, as an editor for both The Wall Street Journal *and* FORTUNE, *I have chronicled the exploits of the high-tech impresarios whose ingenuity transformed the southern reaches of the San Francisco Bay Area into Silicon Valley. It is a frenetic place that thrives on constant change and thus has surprisingly few lasting landmarks.*

And then there is Chef Chu's.

Since opening in 1970, it has been a magnet for many of Silicon Valley's best and brightest, who go there to celebrate business deals with their peers, and to mark special occasions with their families and friends, or just for a nice, intimate meal. Over the years, it struck me that beyond the fact that the food and service are consistently outstanding, another reason Chef Chu's *has built such a loyal following among the high-tech elite is because Chef Chu is a model Silicon Valley entrepreneur himself. This is his story.* —**Brent Schlender**

Forty years ago, at a busy crossroads in the heart of what would soon come to be called Silicon Valley, Lawrence C.C. Chu, a hard-working young Taiwanese immigrant who knew a bit about cooking, opened a tiny takeout shop in a former laundromat. He boldly christened the place *Chef Chu's*.

It was not much more than a hole in the wall, really, with only a few small tables, a short lunch counter, $5,000 worth of used kitchen equipment, and a menu of about 12 entrees. For the plucky 25-year-old entrepreneur and his fiancée Ruth, it represented the first link in what they dreamed

would ultimately become a national chain of hundreds or perhaps even thousands of *Chef Chu's* outlets, the Chinese equivalent of McDonald's.

Like multitudes of other young entrepreneurs in Silicon Valley, Lawrence Chu quickly realized he would need to change his business plan to accommodate the facts on the ground: his customers told him his food was delicious but they preferred a more high-end, family restaurant that offered a cultural experience and a broader menu.

Always a good listener and quick learner, Larry Chu abandoned his fast-food approach and committed to living up to the exalted title of Chef Chu. "Larry didn't really know much about cooking, but he was determined to learn," recalls Ruth. And with that decision, the real Chef Chu was born. To this day, his restaurant, which is known for its creative yet consistent cooking and cuisine and its warm and refined atmosphere, remains an enduring landmark at that very same intersection in the world's epicenter of technological change.

Indeed, Chef Chu blends similar *yin/yang* qualities of leadership that characterize Silicon Valley legends like Steve Jobs of Apple or Gordon Moore of Intel. In the kitchen he is a supremely skilled and imaginative chef, yet the restaurant has succeeded because he's also a savvy businessman and brilliant marketer. He demands the highest esthetic and culinary standards in all aspects of preparing and presenting food, yet he is adored by his employees, many of whom have worked at *Chef Chu's* for decades. He has great respect for the centuries-old traditions of Chinese cuisine, yet he doesn't hesitate to experiment with new ingredients or to apply Chinese techniques to dishes from other cultures. He's a perfectionist with an eye for detail, yet he welcomes suggestions from everyone from the chefs to the patrons.

And then there is his charisma. Like Steve Jobs, Chef Chu is a natural-born performer. He takes the role of the gracious host **very** seriously, genially patrolling his dining rooms throughout the lunch and dinner seatings and taking every opportunity to greet his guests warmly and explain the nuances

Chef Chu (A), grandfather H.T. Chu (B), brother Sampson (C), mother Pai Ming-jeng (D), father H. T. Chu (E), and sister Yolanda Chen (F) in Shanghai, 1947

Chef Chu, a lively 5-year-old, 1948

Parents' wedding day, Chongqing, 1935

of the food they are eating, or to recommend new dishes for them to try. His joy and pleasure are as utterly contagious as they are sincere.

Chef Chu's restaurant has served nearly two million satisfied diners in four decades. Chef Chu has cooked for many heads of state, famous athletes, billionaires, and movie stars. Some of his favorite patrons are the children of all ages for whom he provides lunches in local school cafeterias. He has catered dinners for a thousand people more times than he can count. His famed culinary classes consistently sell out as soon as enrollment opens. And one waits patiently for years to graduate from the waiting list and win a place at the table for his annual Chinese New Year banquet, where he unveils imaginative new twists on traditional Chinese holiday fare.

Chef Chu's is the quintessential Silicon Valley destination restaurant in an area where food fashions seem to come and go as quickly as the business trends. Not only has Chef Chu refined and expanded the repertoire of Chinese cuisine, he has brought an entrepreneurial zeal and a unique esthetic flair to the dining experience. And along the way, he has become one of the world's truly great restaurateurs, helping to hone and redefine the state-of-the-art of modern Chinese cooking and dining.

A CHILD OF WAR
Chef Chu's road to Los Altos was long and winding, but many of those diversions shaped his subsequent success in one way or another. He was born on October 20, 1943, in Chongqing, the largest city in China's Szechuan province, far inland and a world away from more cosmopolitan port cities of Shanghai and Hong Kong. His parents met in Nanjing in the mid-1930s, then moved to Chongqing after Japanese forces occupied Nanjing in the early years of World War II. While the rest of the world celebrated the end of the war in 1945, the long-running Chinese Civil War between Chiang Kai-shek's Republic of China and Mao Zedong's Soviet Republic of China flared up with a vengeance and suddenly Chongqing seemed vulnerable. So the Chus packed

Chef Chu rowing a boat his father built, 1959

Chef Chu and Ruth Ho
on their engagement day, 1970

up and moved to Shanghai, one of the last safe havens for supporters of Chiang Kai-shek. Soon after, the family suffered a tragic misfortune when Chef Chu's mother died suddenly, leaving a heartbroken husband and four children under the age of 6.

Despite the setbacks, Chef Chu's father began to display what might later be called an "entrepreneurial streak." As the Chinese Civil War raged, he combined his skill with a camera with his graphic design capabilities to produce annotated maps of troop movements, cargo shipments, and other wartime logistical phenomena made from his own daily aerial photographs. When the Red Army triumphed in 1949, Chef Chu's father, who was doing similar aerial tracking for a shipping company now, moved his family to safety in Taiwan and then joined them the next year, departing from China on his employers' last freighter to leave Shanghai.

PORTRAIT OF A CHEF AS A YOUNG MAN
Chef Chu's years in Taiwan were blessedly peaceful, although Taiwan at that time had little in the way of urban comforts. Chef Chu's father remarried, and, using his innate design skills, applied the look of classical Chinese palace interiors to tradeshow display systems that could be dismantled and moved from international convention to convention. His work took him around the world to promote Taiwan's young industries, and because he was a skilled photographer, he documented his travels by snapping hundreds of photographs. These fascinating images kindled in his son the twin desires to become a photographer himself and to see as much of the world as possible.

Chef Chu credits his stepmother with awakening his lifelong interest in food. He vividly recalls accompanying her to do the food shopping in Taipei's bustling markets for the big family banquet each Sunday. He would marvel at the colorful arrays of fruits and fish and vegetables, and was mesmerized by the noisy mélange of bargaining and hawking that swirled around him. "My restaurant education started very young," Chef Chu recalls. "My stepmother showed me how to massage a

Modest beginning for what has become a destination restaurant

Restauarant opening day, 1970

Chef Chu, Chef Ho, stepmother Jean Liu, wife Ruth, and family friend Belinda Chung, 1970 chicken to be sure the vendor didn't put rocks in it to make it heavier so he could charge us more. I was raised in an environment where I saw food and business together very early."

When he was 10, he got the capricious idea to leave home and cook snacks to sell on the street. He left home one day undetected, then stopped to purchase a couple of portable stoves for his enterprise. He didn't get very far. Shortly after arriving at the doorstep of a nearby temple where he planned to set up shop, a priest recognized him and took him home. That was the end of his first professional foray into the culinary arts.

When Chef Chu left Taiwan in 1960 to attend school in Hong Kong, he intended to study photography and printing. He lived in a dormitory, and because the food was so bland, he visited the teeming neighborhoods to sample the unbelievable variety of street fare of what was then the most cosmopolitan city in Asia. For nearly four years, he spent as much time eating and exploring the British colony as he did studying. "Hong Kong was where East meets West. There were foods from all over China and all over the world, too," he recalls. "It was the perfect education for a future chef to spend that time of my life there. Hong Kong was where I learned how to eat."

As he would later discover, being autodidactic—smart and resourceful enough to teach oneself—is a crucial trait for an entrepreneur, as well as vital for a chef or artist or creative person of any kind. He also was able to brush-up his English while in the British colony. So his worldly experiences in Hong Kong were ideal basic training for a young man who would next move to San Francisco.

Chef Chu's family had moved to California in 1962, when Mr. Chu was commissioned to design the Taiwan pavilions for the World's Fair in Seattle. In 1963, he moved the family from Los Angeles to San Francisco to oversee the interior design for a renowned restaurant called *Tao Tao* in Chinatown. Chef Chu left Hong Kong to join them in 1964, and just three days after he arrived in the U.S., he interviewed for a job at *Trader Vic's*, a thriving and exot-

Cooking classes began in the restaurant "studio," 1984

Making the most of local ingredients

Filming one of many commercials

A customized truck supports the catering business

14

ic, internationally renowned restaurant. His busboy job gave him a foothold at an establishment where he could learn what it takes to operate a world-class, destination eatery.

Chef Chu worked at *Trader Vic's* for five years in various positions and at two different Bay Area locations, at times filling in at sister restaurants in Los Angeles and Scottsdale, Arizona. The restaurant served cuisine from different parts of Asia, but presented the entrees in ways that more closely resembled European-style restaurants. His *Trader Vic's* apprenticeship taught Chef Chu many of the broad array of skills he would one day need when he ran his own restaurant.

Meanwhile, Chef Chu's father decided to get into the restaurant business for himself. He settled on a suburban setting where there would be less competition: Menlo Park, a quiet but cosmopolitan community near Stanford University. It wasn't long before his *Mandarin House* restaurant was one of the most popular family-style Chinese restaurants in the area.

Soon, Chef Chu was helping out at the family restaurant on his days off, bringing some of the presentation and service esthetics he learned at *Trader Vic's* to the more traditional dining room at the Mandarin House. In 1968, he left *Trader Vic's* to work full time at the family restaurant. But he also returned briefly to Taiwan. It was an eye-opening experience to see the harsh living conditions there. "I made as much money at *Trader Vic's* in one day as some of them made in a month," Chef Chu recalls. "It made me realize how lucky I was to be able to try to make it in America."

So when he returned to the U.S., he attacked his work at the family restaurant with a renewed sense of purpose. The chef at the *Mandarin House* was a venerable old man they called Master Chef Leung. Chef Chu realized that if he wanted to learn to cook like a professional, here was the ideal teacher. He left the dining room behind and joined Master Chef Leung in the kitchen for an intensive course of study that would teach him the fundamentals of Chinese cuisine.

But there was another reason Chef

Chef Chu receives a Five-Star Diamond Award from the American Academy of Restaurant and Hospitality Sciences, 1995

Asian Chefs Association team members Philippe Striffeler (Hotel Nikko), Khai Duong (Ana Mandara) and Chef Chu at the World Culinary Competition in Taiwan

Chu became more concerned about his professional future. In July of 1969, he met Ruth Ho, a beautiful, intelligent, and demure Taiwanese immigrant who was studying economics and accounting at a local college. Soon he realized that to win her attention and the approval of her parents, he would have to demonstrate that he, too, had smarts, self-discipline and ambition. Now, not only did he want to merely learn his way around the kitchen, he wanted to devise a way to have his own restaurant and kitchen.

THE PHILOSOPHER CHEF

When he opened *Chef Chu's* in 1970, Larry Chu quickly realized that there were great virtues in founding a restaurant that not only catered to families but that itself was built on the strength of family relationships. From the beginning, Ruth was key to the success of *Chef Chu's*, critiquing new dishes, suggesting menus, greeting guests, and serving as a mainstay in the business office. When she left the restaurant in 1973 to become a full-time mother, her own mother, Maggie, took over many

of her duties as the restaurant's accountant and business manager. "Ruth was wonderful, but her mother was a one-man army," Chef Chu says. And it took the support of the entire clan to purchase the building that housed the restaurant, a transaction that enabled *Chef Chu's* to grow and expand incrementally, without needing to relocate.

What made *Chef Chu's* unique and fresh forty years ago keeps it unique and fresh today. He liked the idea of having the kitchen close to the diners, so they could watch the cooks in action. To this day, though the restaurant now has multiple dining rooms on two floors, customers can still look into the bustling kitchen as they walk in the front door. What they see is a finely tuned machine humming away. The crew of cooks in smart white chef's tunics collaborate smoothly to produce the scores of *Chef Chu's* signature dishes with an economy of motion that seems choreographed. All the while, waiters in crisp white shirts and trim black vests swoop in and out like clockwork, delivering steaming, glistening plates to the tables literally within

Author Chef Chu meets publisher John F. Kennedy Jr. at Stanford, 1996

Chefs Frank Liou, Lawrence Chu, Chris Yeo & Khai Duong at Glide Memorial Church Benefit

Mikhail Gorbachev with the Chus at their Los Altos home in 2005 seconds after they were prepared.

And then there's the Chef himself, making the rounds of the dining rooms, stopping at each table to inquire if the diners are enjoying the food. He isn't simply being gracious; he's sharing with his customers his epicurean philosophy, both as a culinary artist and as a discriminating consumer of fine food. "If you eat a meal at *Chef Chu's*, you will certainly like it," says Larry Chu Jr., a graduate of UCLA with a degree in economics who is now the partner/manager of his father's establishment. "But if Chef Chu comes to your table and tells you about what went into the creation of that dish, suddenly you'll think, 'This is my favorite dish ever!'"

Chef Chu's cooking philosophy embraces change in many forms. "Part of my job is eating at restaurants of all kinds to get inspiration and to get a feeling for what other chefs are doing," he says. One of the most obvious innovations he has introduced to Chinese cuisine is to present certain dishes as single-serving entrees, rather than in family-style bowls or on large platters.

And he was a *locavore* before such a term existed: "I've always tried to be indigenous in my cooking—using local food products readily available in our area and grown by nearby farmers, so the food reflects the very best in freshness and sustainability." He is always on the lookout for new ingredients that might not be native to China, but that could blossom in new ways when prepared with Chinese methods. "In all cuisines, food does change. At *Chef Chu's* we use ingredients that might not be native to China, but through Chinese cooking techniques we create new dishes with those ingredients."

He wants to educate the next generation's palate as well, so *Chef Chu's* provides lunches to local elementary and middle school students. "How are they going to learn how to enjoy Chinese food if they don't get a good sample of it as children and young people?" he says.

Another of his efforts to evangelize for Chinese cuisine is his pivotal role in the establishment of the Asian Chefs Association, an organization that promotes Asian-inspired cuisine, nurtures

Former Secretary of State George Shultz is a Chef Chu's regular

The choreography in the kitchen is non-stop

developing culinary talent with grants and scholarships, and empowers the Asian culinary community to serve society through special events like the *Chefs Without Borders Annual Holiday Food Drive*.

He also teaches cooking classes to nonprofessionals, relying heavily on his phenomenally successful cookbooks (this is his third). His books have been a magnet for attention nationally; he has appeared frequently on television and radio, and his cooking classes have drawn standing-room-only crowds at department stores—Bloomingdales and Burdines and Filenes, among others—from New York City to Honolulu, and points in between. Frequently he hosts culinary tours of China and Taiwan in which the participants not only eat their way around both lands, but they also learn how Chinese culture and distinctive local ingredients have shaped the cuisine over the centuries.

Like any great artist or entrepre-

neur, Chef Chu never tires of thinking about his work and how to make it better. "He'll wake up in the morning and the first thing we'll talk about is *Chef Chu's*," says his son Larry Jr. "And then after we've both been here all day, and we're closing up shop, and I'm ready to have a beer and unwind a little bit, he'll start in again on the conversation we began the day with: how to improve things around here."

After 40 years, his family and his work have become seamlessly connected. Both Larry Jr., his eldest son, and Jennifer, his younger daughter, who studied hotel and restaurant management at the University of Hawaii, work at *Chef Chu's* full time. (His youngest son, Jon, is a Hollywood film director who has directed two films in the popular the *Step Up* series of urban dance movies, and another daughter, Christina, is in the real estate business. His son Howard lives at home.) "I could never have built *Chef Chu's* without Ruth, and I couldn't have succeeded

Chef Chu with his culinary team and wait staff at the restaurant's 35th anniversary celebration. Front row: Banquet Manager Robert Lam, Catering Manager Joanna Fang, Executive Chef Frank Liou, Chef Chu, Kitchen Manager Jack Lin, Partner/Manager Lawrence Chu Jr., General Manager Charlie Ong, Jennifer Chu-Cruz

if Ruth hadn't been such a wonderful and supportive mother and wife, too" he says.

The Chu family has had its trials; Howard was born with autism, and twice Ruth Chu has had to battle breast cancer. But those misfortunes have served to bring Chef Chu's family closer together. And they also draw strength from the extended family at the restaurant, including patrons who dine there regularly as a vital part of their family routine. So the Chu family genes run deep, and that's a big reason why *Chef Chu's* will live on.

Another reason the restaurant will endure is because in four decades, *Chef Chu's* has become an integral part of the Los Altos community, and not merely because so many customers consider it their favorite dining spot. It also reflects the appreciation for the the Chu family's contributions to the community: Hanging in the restaurant entry are scores of plaques and open letters from hospitals, schools, self-help-centers for the elderly, the YMCA and many other organizations that salute their generosity.

Sitting in a private dining room that also serves as his culinary classroom, he pauses to gaze at an old photograph of his original establishment on the day it opened. Over the years, *Chef Chu's* has grown from one small storefront shop to occupy all of what was once a small shopping center. "I think that most restaurateurs stop growing when they come into their comfort zone," he continues. "But we all know that the lifestyles change, and new ingredients will always become available, and so the food must also change. Eating is like fashion, you know, style." After contemplating for a moment, he adds: "Although the food constantly changes in one way or another, I believe that the basics of what make *Chef Chu's* a good restaurant do not really change. If you love and respect your customers, those basics won't ever change."

Chinese Ingredients *Pictured on pages 20 and 21*

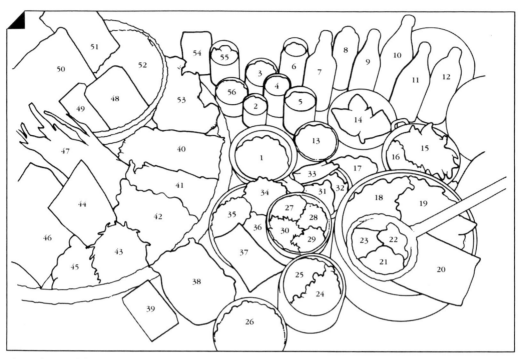

1) quail eggs, 2) button mushrooms, 3) water chestnuts,
4) mushrooms, 5) hoisin sauce, 6) preserved ginger, 7) soy sauce,
8) sesame oil, 9) light soy sauce, 10) and 11) red rice vinegar,
12) rice wine, 13) five-spice powder, 14) bamboo shoots, 15) licorice chips,
16) peanuts, 17) preserved plums, 18) and 19) dried mushrooms,
20) dried seaweed, 21) cardamom seed, 22) dried scallops,
23) sea cucumbers, 24) lotus seeds, 25) black beans, 26) dried shrimp,
27) fennel seeds, 28) crushed chili peppers, 29) and 30) star anise,
31) cardamom seeds, 32) dried abalone, 33) Chinese cinnamon,
34) hair seaweed, 35) black sesame seeds, 36) sesame seeds,
37) pressed bean curd, 38) and 39) tea, 40) rice sticks, 41) dried
Chinese greens, 42) red dates, 43) tiger lily (golden needles),
44) red dates, 45) dried lichee nuts, 46) dried shark's fin, 47) dried
bean curd skins, 48) wheat flour, 49) spicy rice, 50) rice sticks,
51) dried sugar cane, 52) rice, 53) dry noodles, 54) dried bean curd
skins, 55) button mushrooms, 56) shredded bamboo shoots.

Before you begin...

A new cookbook will tempt the confident cook to plunge in immediately with the testing of an interesting recipe. **Please may I ask you to read the following before you begin?**

There are two principles in successful Chinese cooking: **visualizing** the dish before preparation begins and good **timing** during the actual cooking.

To make sure that you are able to **visualize** the dish and the process, we have devised a recipe format which is easy to read, step-by-step. The ingredients appear in the order in which you will need them. If an ingredient is to be marinated, the marinade spices will follow immediately after the ingredient. Preparation instructions are easy to spot and follow the same sequence as the listing of ingredients so that you need not look back and forth. The method of cooking appears in bold—such as steaming, oil blanching, deep-frying, stir-frying—so you can see at a glance how many major steps are involved and the eventual appearance and textures your dish will have. The various methods of preconditioning and cooking are described in detail beginning on page 196. The most valuable information appears on these pages. If I have any "chef's secrets" or tips to pass on, these are the most important.

Please read each recipe carefully, including the notes in which I try to alert you to common pitfalls and there's no need to stumble in them! Also, before you begin, have your serving plate or bowl ready. Having read the recipe, you'll be able to visualize the outcome so select the most appropriate receptacle: If large long pieces of food are involved, select a long plate; if the pieces are round, a round plate; if there are juices, a plate with a lip. Using the appropriate plate in which to serve your dish will add to the success of your presentation. And, with food which requires quick cooking, having the receptacle ready when you remove the pan from the stove is a good idea. The color of ingredients may determine the color of your plate. If there are many colors, and a "busy" feeling is generated, use a white plate. (If Chinese cooking is not infrequent in your home, you might consider adding Chinese tableware to your cupboard. The photographs which appear in this book feature authentic Chinese porcelain in natural, unstylized settings.)

Timing is not just how long the cooking time should be. By timing I mean the ability to cook with your senses.

Use your nose to smell the aroma because the aroma tells you when to proceed. The Chinese will often say, "Bring out the wok aroma, which, literally means cook the green onion and garlic until fragrant." The nose is very important.

Use your eyes to see the color changing or the smoke appearing or the steam rising or the sauce thickening—your eyes will help you create the dish you have envisioned.

Use your ears to hear the rice sizzling or the broth bubbling—to know when to move on to the next step.

And use your mouth to make the ultimate sensory evaluation—to tell you if the spices, seasonings and juices of the ingredients have been properly married and that the best flavor has been achieved.

Learning this kind of timing takes much trial and error, but your common sense and good judgment will always be the ingredients needed to succeed as an accomplished Chinese cook.

L.C.

APPETIZERS

The etiquette of a Chinese dinner party, or of a family meal in a Chinese home, differs greatly from the American tradition. Unlike the Western practice of serving hors d'oeuvres during the social exchanges which precede a meal, Chinese hospitality in a dinner party commences rather promptly at the table.

Since it would not do to bring one's guests to an empty table, several dishes of appetizers are already displayed on the table when guests are seated.

In a banquet setting, the array of appetizers is likely to include at least half a dozen small, delicate dishes with nuts, dried fruits, and little sweet cakes. At a family meal, the appetizers are more likely to include smoked fish, a spicy cold chicken, and colorful arrangements of cold vegetables.

These hot and cold appetizers must be artfully arranged as they offer guests their first view of dinner and promises of the splendid meal which is in store. Their appearance and flavors should stimulate the appetite while pleasing the eye. And, on a more practical note, their presence on the table allows

Every meal should commence with a delightful first course, and Minced Crystal Prawns With Toasted Pine Nuts is an elegant starter (page 27).

guests to begin savoring the meal while the cook attends to the last-minute dishes.

The host may introduce wine at the beginning of the meal and raise the first toast to guests. Chinese wines are distilled from grains and are quite potent. They somewhat resemble whiskey or liquor, and one must acquire a taste for them. I find my guests prefer a nice gewurztraminer or zinfandel!

The appetizers that appear in this section are very versatile—they may be served in the traditional Western style, prior to sitting at the table, and make excellent items for picnics, boat parties, or tailgates. They will give your children great cheer when they find them in lunch boxes, too. Look for other serving suggestions in the notes.

Cold plates are also versatile. Many can be served alone as one-dish meals, such as Lobster with Four Flavors, and make a nice addition to the repertoire of light luncheon fare.

Cold vegetable dishes are also excellent as salads and as condiments to accompany Western meals. Served slightly chilled in the Chinese style, these vegetables are light and crunchy, and enhanced by delicately piquant dressings.

Three or four appetizers or cold plates are a must at a Chinese banquet. They may be skipped in an informal meal, although I would encourage you to tantalize your guests with at least one.

Crab & Cheese Puffs

Crispy, crunchy on the outside, these uniquely-shaped appetizers are so pretty they need no decoration when served. The inside is a delicious, subtle combination of flaked crab meat and softened cream cheese.

Makes: 24 appetizers
Cooking time: 15 minutes

FILLING

- 2 ounces cooked crab meat, lightly flaked (or cooked baby shrimp)
- 1 small package (3 oz.) cream cheese, at room temperature
  Pinch salt
  Pinch white pepper

- 24 won-ton wrappers
  Beaten egg

  Vegetable oil, for deep-frying

  Chinese Hot Mustard Sauce (page 212) and Chef Chu's Dipping Sauce (page 212)

Combine FILLING ingredients well.

To assemble, put 1 teaspoon filling in center of wrapper, seal edges with egg, and fold as illustrated below.

To deep-fry, heat 4 cups oil in wok (or electric deep-fat fryer) to 350°. Fry, a few at a time, for 1½ minutes or until puffy and golden brown. Offer mustard and dipping sauces at the table.

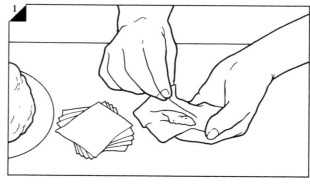

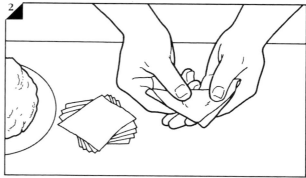

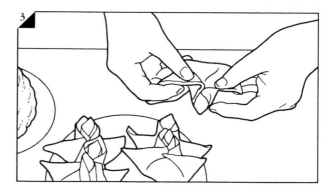

Place 1 teaspoon of filling in center of wrapper and 1) fold to form a triangle. 2) Push filling into center and seal edges together. Lightly brush center of triangle witih beaten egg and 3) bring corners together, forming a butterfly.

Minced Crystal Prawns With Toasted Pine Nuts

This appetizer is the color of delicate porcelain and looks serenely elegant served in a martini glass. The prawns are light and succulent. You are in for an exceptional treat!

Pictured on page 24, 215

Makes: 6 servings
Cooking time: 5 to 10 minutes

- 12 to 14 Belgian endive leaves (separated from 2 to 3 heads), rinsed
- 1 small fresh lotus root, 6 to 7 inches, rinsed, thinly sliced crosswise (see Notes)
- 1 tablespoon cornstarch for dusting

- 1½ cups vegetable oil for deep-frying

FILLING

- ½ pound raw peeled, deveined medium-size prawns (31 to 35 count), rinsed, patted dry
- 4 water chestnuts, peeled
- 1 green onion (white part) minced
- 2 thumb-size ginger slices, minced
- ½ teaspoon salt
- 2 egg whites

- 1 tablespoon chicken broth
- 1 teaspoon dry sherry

- ¼ cup toasted pine nuts or crushed Hunan Candied Pecans (page 43)

Place endive leaves in a bowl of ice water; set aside or refrigerate until needed.

To deep-fry, dust lotus root slices with cornstarch. Heat the oil to 300° in a wok. Add all the lotus root slices to oil and deep-fry for 1½ to 2 minutes until they lose all their moisture; turn until they become golden brown and crisp. Remove and drain on paper towels. Skim off and discard residue from oil. Set oil aside.

To prepare filling, pat shrimp dry. Hand dice prawns finely (smaller than ⅛-inch) with a cleaver. Do not use a food processor. Finely hand-dice water chestnuts. Combine all FILLING ingredients in a large bowl in the order listed, adding egg whites last. Using your hand with fingers curved like a whisk, whip the mixture with your fingers until all pieces become evenly coated with egg whites. The mixture should look smooth and creamy.

To oil-blanch, reheat oil in the wok over medium heat to 300°. (Make sure temperature is correct to prevent browning.) Add FILLING mixture and stir vigorously for 2 minutes to coat each piece with hot oil. Stir until shrimp become separated and turn opaque. Transfer FILLING to a fine strainer set over a heatproof bowl. Drain well.

To stir-fry, remove all but 1 teaspoon of oil from wok; swirl to coat sides. Reheat the wok to 300°. Return shrimp filling. Drizzle in broth and sherry while stirring. Stir vigorously for 30 seconds to coat shrimp evenly. The shrimp will become plump, succulent and moist. Transfer to a small bowl.

To serve in a martini glass, divide filling among 6 glasses. Drain endive leaves, pat dry and arrange two leaves sticking up out of each glass. Top with a few pine nuts. Garnish with 1 lotus root chip. Arrange glass on a plate. Serve remaining lotus root chips in a bowl for munching.

• Notes •

1. We also serve this filling inside trimmed iceberg lettuce, small red radicchio, hearts of romaine, purple endive, and butter lettuce leaves. Garnish as directed.

2. To thinly slice the lotus root crosswise, use a mandoline or cleaver. Deep-frying lotus root chips can be done hours ahead.

Crispy Shrimp Balls

Prawns, fresh ginger, green onion, and bacon are finely chopped together and then shaped into small balls. Each one is rolled in soft, homemade croutons and then deep-fried until lightly golden.

Makes: 20 appetizers
Cooking time: 10 minutes

MIXTURE

- ½ pound medium-size prawns, shelled and deveined
- 1 strip bacon, coarsely chopped
- 1 green onion (white part)
- ¼ teaspoon minced fresh ginger
- 1 water chestnut, coarsely chopped (optional)

SEASONINGS

- 1 egg, slightly beaten
- 3 tablespoons flour
- ½ teaspoon baking powder
- ¼ teaspoon salt
- Pinch white pepper

- 2 cups coarsely-cubed bread croutons

Vegetable oil, for deep-frying

Chinese Hot Mustard Sauce (page 212) and Chef Chu's Dipping Sauce (page 212)

With a food processor or knife, finely chop MIXTURE ingredients until a paste consistency is reached. Add water chestnut and SEASONINGS and mix thoroughly; let stand for 10 minutes.

To shape, dip hand in water (as necessary) to prevent sticking. Grab a handful of mixture (about ¼ cup) and squeeze out 1-inch balls from the top of your fist as illustrated below. Roll each ball in a tray filled with bread croutons, covering completely. Lightly squeeze outside of ball so that croutons stick; set aside.

To deep-fry, heat 3 or 4 cups oil in wok to 275°. Add balls, all at once, and then raise oil temperature to 350°. Continue frying for 2 to 4 minutes or until golden brown. Remove and drain on paper towels.

To serve, arrange on serving platter with small bowls of mustard and dipping sauces at the table.

• Notes •

1. To make fresh croutons, trim crusts from 4 slices bread and then cut into cubes about ¼-inch thick. Allow them to dry for about 5 minutes in a 300° oven.

2. If using a food processor to prepare paste, use steel knife blade and only process for about 1 minute.

3. This is almost a double-frying process. The balls cook at a lower temperature to retain their shape as well as heat the inside; the higher temperature is required to brown the outside.

Dip hand in water to prevent sticking. Then 1) grab handful of mixture and squeeze out 1-inch balls from top of fist. With spoon, lower balls into tray and 2) roll them in croutons to cover evenly.

Phoenix Tail Fried Prawns

These butterflyed prawns, quickly deep-fried to be crunchy on the outside but succulent and flavorful inside, are worthy of their majestic name. Serve with my special dipping sauce.

Makes: 26 to 30 appetizers
Cooking time: 20 to 30 minutes

1 pound medium-size
(26–30 count) prawns

BATTER
1 cup flour
⅓ cup cornstarch
1 cup water
1 egg
2 tablespoons oil
½ teaspoon baking powder
Pinch salt

MARINADE
¼ teaspoon salt
Pinch garlic powder
Pinch white pepper

Vegetable oil, for deep-frying

Lemon slices
Chinese Hot Mustard
Sauce (page 212) and
Chef Chu's Dipping Sauce
(page 212)

Mix together BATTER ingredients until the consistency of heavy cream. Let stand ½ hour.

Shell prawns, leaving tails attached. Split down the back, removing black vein, to butterfly. Rinse in cold water to clean thoroughly, drain and pat dry.

Combine MARINADE ingredients with prawns and let stand for 10 minutes.

To deep-fry, heat 4 cups oil in wok (or electric deep-fat fryer) to 300°. Grab prawns by the tail, dip into batter to coat, and drop into oil. Deep-fry, a few at a time, for 2 minutes. When all prawns have been fried, increase oil to 350°. Return prawns, all at once, to oil and deep fry 1½ to 2 minutes longer until golden brown. Remove with strainer and drain on paper towels.

To serve, arrange prawns decoratively on platter and garnish with lemon slices at both ends of platter. Serve with mustard and dipping sauces at table.

• *Notes* •

1. If you want to make prawns ahead of time, deep-fry just once until lightly browned; then do the second frying at serving time.

2. When choosing fresh prawns, look for ones with a light grey-blue tinge to the shell and translucent flesh.

Grilled Honey-glazed Quail With Watercress Salad

We serve this quail as an elegant appetizer at banquets. It looks beautiful presented over a fresh green watercress salad tossed with a light lime dressing. You'll love the flavors! *Pictured on facing page*

Makes: 8 servings
Cooking time: about 8 minutes under broiler or 4 to 5 minutes on a barbecue grill

8 fresh quail (or semi-boneless quail), halved lengthwise

MARINADE

¼ cup oyster sauce
¼ cup honey
¼ cup oil
1 tablespoon sugar
1 teaspoon salt
½ teaspoon black pepper
6 garlic cloves, minced
12 sprigs Chinese parsley (cilantro)

LIME DRESSING

2 tablespoons white vinegar
2 tablespoons water
2 tablespoons fish sauce
2 tablespoons Kikkoman Thai Chili Sauce
2 teaspoons lime juice (¼ lime)
2 teaspoons sugar
2 garlic cloves, finely minced
½ fresh red jalapeño chile, seeded, very finely minced

SALAD

1 bunch watercress, washed, heavy stems removed, drained well
12 cherry or grape tomatoes

Rinse quail, drain and pat dry. Set aside.

Combine MARINADE ingredients in a blender. Process until finely minced. Transfer to a bowl. Set aside half of the MARINADE for basting. Cover and refrigerate. Brush or dip each quail piece into the remaining MARINADE, coating both sides generously. Place quail on a platter and cover with plastic. Chill 1 hour or overnight.

Combine LIME DRESSING ingredients in a bowl. Place SALAD ingredients in another bowl. Cover both separately and refrigerate until needed. (Can be prepared up to a few hours ahead.)

To broil, line a rimmed baking sheet with aluminum foil. Place a grill rack on top of the foil to hold quail above cooking juices and produce grill marks. Place quail, skin-side up in a single layer on the grill. Brush with reserved MARINADE. Broil 6 to 7 inches from broiling element for 3 minutes until browned. Turn quail skin-side down, brush with MARINADE and broil another 3 minutes until quail is browned. Quail should be juicy inside and browned well on both sides. The quail is best eaten and served right after cooking.

To grill on an outdoor barbecue, place quail on an oiled grill grate set over a medium-hot flame or coals. Grill for 3 to 4 minutes on each side to establish grill marks. Remove from grill when each piece is finished cooking. Keep warm.

To serve, toss SALAD lightly with LIME DRESSING. Divide SALAD among individual serving plates. Place two quail halves, skin-side up leaning against each other, over salad greens. The quail is best served right after grilling.

• Note •

Using semi-boneless quail saves time and work. Because they have less bone structure, they must be skewered to lie flat and to be turned on the grill. They are lovely served as appetizers, placed on a banana leaf-lined platter with the salad served on the side.

Swordstick Beef

If your party is outdoors, here's a perfect way to involve your guests. These marinated appetizers allow your friends to gather around one or more hibachis or grills and cook at their pleasure.

Makes: 24 appetizers
Cooking time: 10 minutes

1 pound flank steak, sliced against grain ¼- by 1- by 2-inches thick

MARINADE

3 tablespoons soy sauce
2 teaspoons dry sherry
2 tablespoons Hoisin sauce
1 green onion (white part), minced
1 tablespoon vegetable oil
1 teaspoon sesame oil
 Pinch white pepper

24 six-inch bamboo skewers
3 tablespoons vegetable oil (for pan-frying only)

Combine MARINADE ingredients in a bowl; add beef strips and mix well. Let stand for about 20 minutes. Lift out strips and thread 3 or 4 pieces on each skewer (reserve marinade for grilling).

To grill, arrange skewers on grill over hot coals and cook, rotating frequently and basting with marinade, for 1 to 2 minutes or until desired doneness is reached.

Or, to **pan-fry,** set wok over high heat for 1 minute until hot. Add oil and swirl pan to coat sides. When oil is hot, lay beef skewers around sides of wok; cook, turning often and basting with oil, until desired doneness is reached.

• *Notes* •

1. You'll be able to slice the beef easily if you partially freeze it first.

2. Use reserved marinade rather than vegetable oil for basting when cooking on a grill over hot coals.

34

New Moon Spring Rolls

This variation on traditional spring rolls uses tender winter bamboo shoots, available at the end of Chinese New Year when the first New Moon of Spring appears on the lunar calendar, to make a fresh and delicate appetizer.

Makes: 24
Cooking time: 20 to 25 minutes

FILLING

- ¼ cup bacon or ham, julienned
- 6 to 10 fresh black mushrooms, julienned
- 1 (1 pound 3.5 ounce) can winter bamboo shoots (Ma Ling Brand), drained, julienned
- ½ cup cooked shrimp
- ½ teaspoon sesame oil
- 1 cup Chinese yellow chives, cut in 2-inch lengths
- 2 tablespoons vegetable oil

SEASONING SAUCE

- 2 tablespoons chicken broth
- 1 tablespoon soy sauce
  Pinch salt
- ¼ teaspoon white pepper

  Flour paste (3 tablespoons flour to 3 tablespoons water, mixed together)

- 1 (1 pound) package spring roll wrappers, 8 x 8 inch

- 1 quart vegetable oil for deep-frying

  Worcestershire sauce or Chef Chu's Dipping Sauce (page 212)

Prepare FILLING ingredients; set aside.

Combine SEASONING SAUCE in a small bowl.

To stir-fry, heat 2 tablespoons of oil in a wok until hot. Add bacon or ham and stir-fry for 1 minute over high until bacon pieces separate. Add mushrooms and bamboo shoots and stir for 1 minute. Add SEASONING SAUCE and shrimp; toss vigorously. The filling should be slightly moist. Stir in sesame oil. Remove from heat and stir in yellow chives. Transfer FILLING to a colander to drain off extra moisture. Set aside to cool or refrigerate.

To assemble, place a wrapper on a flat surface with one corner pointed toward you. Place 2 tablespoons FILLING on the nearest corner. Spread filling into a compact 3-inch length. Roll the corner nearest you over the filling twice to enclose it completely. Fold the side corners in over the filling; continue rolling tightly toward the opposite corner. Before you get to the corner, dab a little flour paste along the edges. Finish rolling to seal edges. Place apart on a tray in a single layer.

To deep-fry, heat 1 quart oil in a clean wok to 365°. Deep-fry 6 to 8 rolls at a time until golden brown on all sides, turning rolls to brown evenly. Remove and drain. Reheat oil before each batch. Repeat process with remaining rolls.

To serve individually, cut rolls in half diagonally. Place cut side up, standing on a plate or present on a banana leaf or lettuce-lined platter. Serve with Worcestershire sauce or Chef Chu's Dipping Sauce (page 212).

• *Note* •

For a vegetarian alternative, omit the ham and shrimp and increase the mushrooms or add shredded or julienned celery or carrot in place of the meat.

Crispy Tofu Bites   *Pictured on page 144*

This easy appetizer, seasoned with Five-spice Salt, can also serve as a tasty vegetarian main course.

Makes: 4 to 6 servings
Cooking time: 15 minutes

- 1 (1 pound) block of medium-firm tofu

  Oil for deep-frying

SPICES
- 1 tablespoon minced ginger
- 1 fresh red jalapeño or serrano chile, minced
- 2 green onions, chopped
- $\frac{1}{3}$ small yellow onion, chopped

- 2 teaspoons Five-spice Salt (page 212)

- 1 tablespoon sesame oil

Drain tofu of water and pat dry. Cut tofu block into 1-inch cubes.

To deep-fry, heat 2 cups oil to 365° in a wok. Deep-fry half the tofu cubes in a single layer, turning to brown all sides until a golden crust is formed. Remove and drain. Repeat with remaining tofu.

To stir-fry, remove all but 1 tablespoon oil from wok. Reheat oil until smoking. Add SPICES and stir for 45 seconds until onion is lightly browned. Add tofu and gently toss to lightly coat. Add sesame oil and toss lightly.

To serve, transfer to a platter or individual small plates. Can be served or passed as an appetizer with toothpicks.

Szechuan Pickled Cucumber Spirals *Pictured on page 144*

These intriguing spiral pickles are refreshing and one of the most requested appetizers in the restaurant. Their spicy, sweet-tart taste stimulates the appetite and balances off richer appetizers to usher in a great meal.

Makes: 8 to 12 servings
Cooking time: 5 minutes

- 1 tablespoon salt
- 12 pickling cucumbers, small diameter and 6 to 7 inches long (or 2 Japanese cucumbers)

PICKLING SOLUTION

- 3 cups water
- 7 tablespoons sugar
- 1 tablespoon salt
- ½ cup white distilled vinegar

SPICES

- 2 red jalapeño or serrano chilies, thinly sliced
- 5 slices ginger, finely shredded
- 3 tablespoons hot chili oil

• *Notes* •

1. Alternate Cutting Method: Make cucumber sticks using an English cucumber. Remove seeds with a spoon, then cut into 2- to 3-inch long sticks about ½-inch thick. Salt, rinse and pat dry as directed. Assemble with PICKLING SOLUTION and refrigerate. Serve sticks from the jar.

2. Use crisp, firm cucumbers available during the season. I recommend small pickling cucumbers or small-diameter, firm English cucumbers. Serve them on a cold plate with other appetizers.

Sprinkle 1 tablespoon salt over pickling cucumbers in a bowl. Lightly mix. Let stand 30 minutes.

To make cucumber spirals, roll each cucumber under the palm of your hand on a cutting board to loosen up and soften the cucumber. Cut off a ½ inch from each end of the cucumber. Hold a cleaver parallel to the cutting board about $1/8$-inch from the surface. Parallel-cut the cucumber $1/8$-inch thick while pressing down and rolling the cucumber along the board with your other hand, making a single $1/8$-inch-thick sheet of cucumber. Roll the cucumber back into its original shape making a spiral-shaped roll. Place cucumbers in a bowl and cover with cold water. Set aside for 30 minutes. Rinse off all salt from rolls, inside and outside, and pat dry.

Meanwhile, combine PICKLING SOLUTION ingredients together in a non-reactive stainless steel pan and bring to a boil. Remove from heat and cool. Stir in SPICES. (This can be done ahead and set aside.)

To assemble, pour cooled pickling solution into a non-reactive container, glass jar or ceramic pickling crock. Add cucumbers and stir to mix. Cover container with a non-reactive cover. Refrigerate at least 4 hours or overnight to allow flavors to develop. (Refrigerated pickles will keep up to a month in PICKLING SOLUTION.)

To serve, cut each cylinder crosswise into 1-inch-thick pieces. Place cucumber, cutside up showing spiral, on a serving plate. Garnish top with pickled red jalapeño chilies.

Phoenix Wings

Simple drumsticks easily become the dramatic wings of the mythical bird. Very popular, you'd be well-advised to double the quantity.

Makes: 12 appetizers
Cooking time: 15 minutes

6 chicken wings

MARINADE
1 green onion (white part), minced
¼ teaspoon minced fresh ginger
1 tablespoon dry sherry
½ teaspoon salt
   Pinch curry powder
1 egg
¼ cup cornstarch

   Vegetable oil, for deep-frying

   Sweet & Sour Sauce (page 213) or Lemon Sauce (page 69)

Break chicken wing at joint; twist joint, inside out, to expose bone. Separate to make 2 pieces. Cut off wing tip, remove smaller bone; push meat to end of remaining bone creating a "drumstick" as illustrated below.

Combine MARINADE ingredients with chicken in the order listed and let stand for 10 minutes.

To deep-fry, heat 4 cups oil in a wok (or electric deep-fat fryer) to 350°. Add chicken and fry for 8 to 10 minutes or until golden brown. Remove and drain.

To serve, arrange drumsticks in a circle on serving plate. Place sauce in a small bowl in center.

• *Notes* •

1. For easier handling, hold chicken wings with a towel while breaking the joint.

2. Chinese gourmets consider the chicken wing the tastiest part of the chicken—the meat is sweet, has substance, yet is tender.

3. Phoenix wings are great for picnics, and a nice treat in school lunch boxes.

1) Using a towel to prevent slipping, break chicken wing at joint. 2) Twist joint, inside out to expose bone, and push meat down to end, creating a "drumstick."

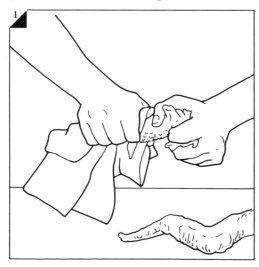

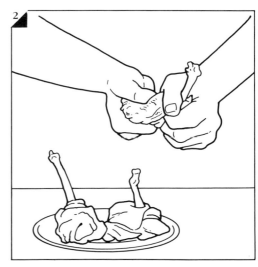

Chinese Barbecued Pork

This colorful, red-glazed pork makes many appearances in the Chinese diet—as a delectable snack, as a bright garnish in soups, on dumplings, or in fried rice. If you are in Chinatown, don't resist the temptation to try the freshly cooked barbecued pork on display. This recipe calls for the pork to be oven-roasted just like the original Cantonese specialty.

Makes: 40 to 50 appetizers
Cooking time: 1 hour

1½ to 2 pounds pork shoulder butt, trimmed and cut into 2- by 2- by 5-inch-size strips

MARINADE

¼ cup light soy sauce or ½ teaspoon salt
1 tablespoon dry sherry
½ teaspoon Chinese five-spice
½ teaspoon garlic powder
¼ teaspoon curing salt (optional)

COATING

½ cup catsup
½ cup sugar
½ teaspoon salt
½ teaspoon red food coloring (optional)
¼ teaspoon egg yellow food coloring (optional)

Toasted sesame seeds

Chinese Hot Mustard Sauce (page 212) and Chef Chu's Dipping Sauce (page 212)

Combine MARINADE ingredients and rub into meat. Cover and allow to stand for at least 2 hours or preferably overnight.

Combine COATING ingredients and mix with meat. Set aside for 2 hours.

To roast, preheat oven to 350°. Pour 1 cup water in a roasting pan. Remove pork from sauce (reserve for basting) and lay strips on a rack. Set rack in pan close to but not touching the water. Roast for 30 minutes, brushing occasionally with reserved sauce. Turn strips over, baste again, and continue roasting for 30 minutes longer.

To serve, sprinkle sesame seeds lightly on top of sliced pork and offer mustard and dipping sauces at the table.

• Notes •

1. I recommend using pork shoulder butt rather than the more common pork butt because it has a greater proportion of lean meat.

2. Slightly frozen meat is easier to cut into strips.

3. Chinese barbecued pork is an ingredient in many other recipes. Try doubling the recipe and freezing the extra pork for later use. It will keep for several months in the freezer.

4. Good in sandwiches, too.

5. For barbecued spareribs, substitute 2 to 3 pounds meaty ribs for pork butt. Score surface of ribs and cut into sections; marinate and roast as directed.

Five-spice Beef

Originating in Northern China, this dish was practically considered a staple food because the spices used preserved the meat and therefore made refrigeration unnecessary. A different version found in the Southern part of China uses this beef as a filling for dumplings similar to ravioli.

In a restaurant, the Master Sauce is very important. It's similar to a sourdough starter in that if properly treated, it can be used and added to for many years. Traditionally, it's offered as a gift to someone just beginning as a homemaker.

Makes: 8 to 10 servings
Cooking time: 2 hours

- 2 beef shanks (1–1½ lbs. each) or 2 or 3 pounds bottom round
- 1 teaspoon salt
- 1 teaspoon Szechuan peppercorns
- 1 tablespoon dry sherry
- ¼ teaspoon curing salt (optional)

MASTER SAUCE

- 4 quarts water
- 2 knobs fresh ginger, crushed
- 4 green onions, tied in knots

In a cheesecloth bag put:
- 6 star anise
- 1 teaspoon Szechuan peppercorns
- 1 teaspoon fennel seed
- 2 pieces preserved tangerine peel
- 5 cardamom seeds
- ½ teaspoon whole cloves

- 1½ cups dark soy sauce
- ½ cup sugar
  Dash sesame oil
  Chinese parsley (cilantro)

Prick meat all over with a fork. Rub in salt, Szechuan peppercorns, sherry, and curing salt. Let stand for 1 hour.

In a deep pot, bring water to a boil. Add MASTER SAUCE ingredients including cheesecloth bag. Reduce heat and simmer, uncovered, for about 30 minutes. Stir in soy sauce and sugar; keep warm.

To water-blanch, put beef in boiling water and blanch for 3 minutes. Remove and drain, discarding any peppercorns sticking to sides; then add to master sauce. Bring mixture to a boil, reduce heat, cover, and simmer for 1 to 1½ hours. Remove meat from sauce (reserve sauce for other uses) and refrigerate until cold.

To serve, cut meat across the grain in ⅛-inch-thick slices. Arrange decoratively on platter, sprinkle with sesame oil, and garnish with parsley leaves.

• Notes •

1. You can adjust the flavor of the MASTER SAUCE to suit your own taste by increasing or decreasing the amounts of spices and seasonings.

2. Serve this cold by itself, or as part of any combination cold plate.

3. It's important to remove the cheesecloth bag before storing the MASTER SAUCE. If properly cared for, the sauce can be reused over and over (for more information, see page 198 and 205).

4. Try it in sandwiches or as a buffet cold cut.

Hunan Candied Pecans

This dish calls for your keen eye—first to judge color when deep-frying, then to appreciate the rich glaze when finished. Here is a Hunan delicacy and an elegant snack.

Makes: 4 cups
Cooking time: 20 minutes

1 pound fresh pecans, shelled
2 quarts boiling water

COATING
½ cup water
1 cup sugar
Pinch salt

Vegetable oil, for deep-frying

To water-blanch, drop pecans into boiling water for 2 minutes and then drain.

To coat, heat COATING ingredients in a wok until boiling. Mix in pecans, reduce heat to medium, and cook for about 5 minutes. Stir vigorously and watch carefully so that sugar doesn't burn. When sugar is completely dissolved and becomes carmelized, remove pecans and pour into strainer to drain off excess sugar.

To deep-fry, immediately heat 1½ quarts oil in clean wok to 300°. Add pecans, and cook for 5 minutes, stirring often. Raise temperature gradually to 350°; pecans will reach a deep chocolate-brown color and will start to float to the surface.

Remove, drain well, and place in a shallow pan to cool. Shake pan often to prevent pecans from sticking. When coating turns glossy, blot pecans with paper towels to remove excess oil. When completely cooled, store nuts in a tightly-sealed container or plastic bag in refrigerator or cool place.

• *Notes* •

1. The purpose of blanching is to remove the pecans' bitterness as well as bleach their color.

2. Deep-frying first at 300° gets rid of any moisture remaining in the pecans; raising the temperature to 350° enables the sugar to form a glaze on the outside.

3. Deep-frying at the right oil temperature is the key to success—if the temperature is too high in the beginning, the pecans will burn right away.

4. I don't recommend using an electric deep-fat fryer since the temperature is difficult to control.

Shanghai Smoked Fish

Not smoked at all, this recipe typifies the unique style found in Chinese cooking. First deep-fried then braised in a spicy anise sauce, the snapper takes on a smoky look during cooking. This fish is so unique, guests never seem to have enough of it.

Makes: 6 to 8 servings
Cooking time: 30 minutes

2 pounds fish steaks (rock cod, halibut, or red snapper)

MARINADE

2 tablespoons soy sauce
1 tablespoon dry sherry
5 thumb-size slices fresh ginger, crushed
2 green onions, cut in pieces

Vegetable oil, for deep-frying

SPICES

2 tablespoons vegetable oil
1 teaspoon Szechuan peppercorns
2 star anise
4 thumb-size slices fresh ginger
1 green onion, cut in pieces

1½ cups water or Rich Chicken Broth (page 52)

SEASONINGS

3 tablespoons soy sauce
1 tablespoon dry sherry
3 tablespoons sugar
¼ teaspoon salt

2 teaspoons white vinegar
¼ teaspoon Chinese five-spice
½ teaspoon sesame oil

Chinese parsley (cilantro)

Combine MARINADE ingredients and rub onto fish. Let stand 10 minutes.

To deep fry, heat 2 cups oil in a wok (or electric deep-fat fryer) to 375°. Cook fish in batches, maintaining oil temperature, for 5 to 7 minutes or until dark brown on outside yet firm inside. Remove fish and drain, discarding oil.

To braise, heat wok over high heat for about 1 minute until hot. Add 2 tablespoons oil and swirl to coat sides. When oil is hot, add remaining SPICES and cook until fragrance emerges. Add water, bring to a boil, and cook over medium heat for 5 minutes. Add SEASONINGS, bring to boil, and continue cooking for about 5 minutes more.

Add fish to sauce, mixing gently to coat. Stir in vinegar and Chinese five-spice. Continue cooking 5 more minutes, stirring gently and constantly, until sauce thickens. Stir in sesame oil, remove from heat, and cool to room temperature. Cover and refrigerate until serving.

To serve, remove fish from sauce, discarding any spices clinging to sides, and transfer to serving platter. Garnish with leaves of Chinese parsley.

• Notes •

1. Serve as a cold plate, or on top of Fresh Noodles (page 162), or in a soup.

2. Normally you can reuse oil after deep-frying; however, in this recipe the oil becomes dark and odorous, so discard it.

Shanghai Braised Black Mushrooms

There is no flavor that rivals the woodsy, subtly aromatic black mushroom. Although most frequently used in combination with other vegetables and meats, here it stands alone braised in sherry, soy, and a dash of sesame oil. Delicious cold and hot.

Makes: 6 to 8 servings
Cooking time: 30 minutes

2 dozen large dried black mushrooms
3 tablespoons vegetable oil
6 thumb-size slices fresh ginger
2 green onions (including tops), cut in pieces

SAUCE
5 tablespoons soy sauce
2 tablespoons dry sherry
1½ cups Rich Chicken Broth (page 52), or chicken bouillon
1 tablespoon sugar
1 tablespoon sesame oil

Presoak mushrooms in warm water for 20 to 30 minutes. Drain and remove stems.

To braise, heat wok over high heat for about 1 minute until hot. Add oil and swirl to coat sides. When hot, add ginger and onions and cook for 30 seconds until fragrant. Stir in SAUCE ingredients and then add mushrooms. Bring to a boil, reduce heat, and simmer, stirring occasionally to prevent burning, for 20 minutes or until liquid is absorbed. Mix in sesame oil, remove from heat, and cool.

To serve, discard ginger and green onion. Arrange mushrooms, cap-side up, on platter or as part of any combination cold plate.

Variation: Black Mushrooms & Bamboo Shoots (Winter Delicacy). Just before braising mushrooms, add 1 cup bamboo shoots, cut into bite-size pieces using rolling cut (page 194).

• *Notes* •

1. Mushrooms should be just as soft and dark on the outside as inside when completely cooked.

2. This dish is wonderful when served hot, too. A good accompaniment to roast meats.

3. Don't stir in the mushrooms before the sauce because they will toughen.

Spicy Hot Garlic Chicken

Delightful in summertime, my highly-spiced, Szechuan-style chicken is served cold as an appetizer at the restaurant. However, some of my students tell me they enjoy serving it as an entrée as well.

Makes: 8 to 10 servings
Cooking time: 30 minutes

1 broiler-fryer chicken (about 3 lbs.)

SAUCE
2 teaspoons minced fresh ginger
2 small cloves garlic, minced or pressed
2 green onions (including tops), minced
⅓ cup soy sauce
2 teaspoons hot Chili Oil, page 212 or purchased
3 tablespoons red rice vinegar
1½ tablespoons sugar
1 teaspoon sesame oil
Pinch freshly ground roasted Szechuan peppercorns (page 212)

Chinese parsley (cilantro)

To cook, place chicken in enough boiling water to cover and cook for 10 minutes. Turn off heat and let stand for 10 minutes more. Remove chicken, rinse under cold water, and refrigerate until cold.

Bone chicken completely, except for wings, keeping meat in large pieces and leaving skin on. Slice meat ½-inch thick and reassemble on serving platter to recreate original shape (see illustration, page 85).

To serve, combine SAUCE ingredients well in a bowl and spoon over chicken. Garnish with parsley leaves.

Variation: Mild Onion Chicken. For a milder sauce, combine 2 teaspoons minced fresh ginger, 1 minced green onion (including top), 1 tablespoon salt, and ½ cup vegetable oil. Spoon over chicken as directed above.

• Notes •

1. Yes, chicken will cook through by using this rapid boiling and steeping method. Make sure the water is boiling before immersing the chicken completely. Do not overcook.

2. This dish keeps well. Try any leftover chicken as topping for soup noodles.

Lobster With Four Flavors

Thin slices of perfectly cooked lobster are surrounded by four tantalizing sauces for dipping. A dish for a banquet, a meal in itself, or a new way to serve your catch at a beach party.

Makes: 6 to 8 servings
Cooking time: 30 minutes

- 2 lobster tails (10 oz. each), or 2 whole California lobsters

- 2 cucumbers diagonally sliced 1/8-inch thick

- 1/2 teaspoon salt

  Bamboo skewers

GINGER SAUCE
Page 213

HOT & SPICY SAUCE
Page 213

PONG-PONG SAUCE
Page 213

CHEF CHU'S DIPPING SAUCE
Page 212

Insert skewers lengthwise through lobster tails to prevent curling. Cover lobster with water, bring to a boil, and cook for 8 to 10 minutes. Drain, remove skewers, and refrigerate.

Meanwhile, mix cucumber slices with salt and let stand 15 minutes. Drain well and refrigerate.

In four separate bowls, combine ingredients for GINGER SAUCE (page 213), HOT & SPICY SAUCE (page 213), PONG-PONG SAUCE (page 213), and CHEF CHU'S DIPPING SAUCE (page 212).

To serve, remove and discard lobster shells; slice meat 1/4-inch thick. Overlap cucumber slices to form a circular bed in center of serving platter. Arrange lobster slices on bed, leaving the decorative tips of the cucumber showing. Place two bowls of sauce at each side of platter to serve.

Variation: Prawns With Four Flavors.

Cook 1 pound of prawns (21–25 count) in boiling water; drain, shell, and split in half lengthwise. Arrange on platter, tails out, on bed of cucumbers and serve with the four sauces.

• *Notes* •

1. English cucumbers (water-blanched) or bean sprouts may be substituted for cucumbers.

2. This would make a delightful meal in itself, for luncheon parties or a summertime supper.

Pong-pong Chicken

"Pong-pong" means stick and the name of this dish suggests that the tender chicken became so because it had had a beating. The julienned strips of chicken also resemble match sticks—so take your choice. Most Chinese dishes bear names that describe their appearance or method of cooking. Eating is a straightforward, serious business! And this recipe for Pong-pong chicken is seriously hot and delicious.

Makes: 6 to 8 servings
Cooking time: 30 minutes

---

2 cups cooked chicken
   meat
2 cups bean sprouts

SAUCE
3 tablespoons peanut butter
   or sesame paste
3 tablespoons soy sauce
1½ teaspoons sugar
3 tablespoons chicken
   broth
1 teaspoon minced fresh
   ginger
1 green onion (white part),
   minced
1 clove garlic, minced or
   pressed
1 tablespoon red rice
   vinegar
1 tablespoon hot Chili Oil,
   page 212 or purchased
1½ teaspoons sesame oil

   Chinese parsley (cilantro)

Shred cold chicken into match-stick-size pieces; set aside.

To water blanch, cook bean sprouts in boiling water for 1 minute; run under cold water and drain.

Combine SAUCE ingredients thoroughly. Arrange bean sprouts on serving platter and cover with shredded chicken; refrigerate until cold.

To serve, spoon sauce over chicken and garnish with Chinese parsley leaves.

• Note •

You can substitute either regular or English cucumbers for bean sprouts. Shred as directed but do not water-blanch.

Buddhist Vegetarian Chicken

The Buddhist philosophy, which reveres all creatures, is the source of a widely popular school of cuisine featuring vegetarian dishes. Nutritious, they are deceptive, too, as many are designed to imitate meats, such as this delicate concoction of soy bean curd skins flavored with onion and soy sauce, then steamed, cooled, and cut into pieces that resemble thin slices of chicken.

Makes: 6 to 8 servings
Cooking time: 2 hours

- 4 large frozen bean curd skins (page 200), thawed

MIXTURE
- 1 green onion (including top), minced
- ⅓ cup soy sauce
- 1 small piece fermented bean curd
- 1 teaspoon sugar
- 1 tablespoon sesame oil

  String
  Sesame oil
  Vegetable flower
  (optional)

Combine MIXTURE ingredients in a small bowl to form a paste.

To assemble, lay 2 flat sheets of bean curd on top of each other. Brush surface with half of the mixture. Fold 3 sides of the sheet into the center, then roll up jelly-roll fashion toward the non-folded edge. Continue rolling almost to edge but then fold that edge back onto roll so that sauce is not forced out. Wrap string, diagonally, around roll 4 or 5 times; secure at end and then reverse process and wrap back, 4 or 5 times, to original starting point. Secure tightly. Repeat for second roll.

To steam, place both rolls on rack in steamer; cover and steam over boiling water for 2 hours. Allow to cool.

To serve, cut off string and cut each roll diagonally into 1-inch pieces. Sprinkle with sesame oil and garnish with vegetable flower, if desired.

• Notes •

1. You'll find bean curd skins in frozen section of Oriental markets.

2. In addition to the soy mixture, try spreading sheets with chopped dried shrimp or preserved mustard green *(jah choy)* before rolling.

SOUPS

A formal Chinese meal may involve ten or more courses, and the sequence in which they are served is surprisingly different from a Western-style meal. Soup may be served last, between courses to clear the palate, or to indicate the end of many courses. At an informal family meal, soup often appears along with the main dishes.

Chinese soups are varied—from the light, clear Egg Flower Soup, to the pungent Hot & Sour Soup, to the delicately prepared Fish Blossom Soup. Soups can offer drama to your dinner, too. To draw exclamations from your guests, try Kabocha Bisque with Fat Choy Purses. The colorful bisque can be served by itself for a simple family dinner, but can be easily elevated to a special occasion by adding the Purses for their symbolic meaning. Fresh Ginger Clam Soup is simple and easy to make, and is a must when fresh Manila clams are available. Enjoy the fresh taste of clams in a clear bracing broth of ginger and white pepper.

While many other ethnic cuisines offer a variety of their soups cold, Chinese generally prefer their soup piping hot. The recipes that follow offer some of the very best among a wide variety of soups we serve. When preparing any soup, I *insist* that you start with a delicious homemade stock such as Rich Chicken Broth. Am I emphatic enough?

After making a rich broth (which can be done well in advance and in large batches), proceed with the remaining instructions for slicing, dicing, or shredding meat or fresh vegetables, which can be completed rather swiftly.

A quick glance at a recipe will give you an idea which soups are simple to prepare and which ones require more patience. Check through the notes for suggestions on how much can be done in advance. Several soups are "show stoppers"! They can serve as the centerpiece of your menu so you can plan a fairly simple meal around that one soup and save time and energy.

Soup stimulates one's appetite for the feast to come. Ginger Clam Soup (page 65) is a colorful and healthy way to warm up.

Fish Blossom Soup   *Pictured on facing page*

Popular in Taiwan, this festive soup becomes the star attraction when brought to the table. Hot chicken broth is poured (carefully) over thin slices of raw fish fillets, fried won-ton wrappers, and pieces of lettuce. It's an unusually beautiful soup to prepare because once the broth is poured, the fish turns white and flaky as it cooks before your eyes.

(A word of caution: don't dump the broth in all at once and don't pour it from very high up. I did *both* the first time we tried to take the picture. I splattered liquid all over, ruining the satin tablecloth and was not asked to try again when this photo was shot.)

Makes: 8 servings
Cooking time: 10 minutes

- 5 won-ton wrappers
- 1 rock cod or red snapper fillet (about ½ lb.), skinned
- 2 quarts Rich Chicken Broth (page 52), or chicken bouillon

SEASONINGS

- 1 tablespoon dry sherry
  Salt and white pepper to taste

- ¼ head Iceberg lettuce, torn into bite-size pieces
- 2 thumb-size slices fresh ginger, finely shredded
- 1 green onion (white part), finely shredded
- 1 tablespoon sesame seeds, crushed
- 1 tablespoon roasted peanuts, crushed

Cut each won-ton wrapper into four triangles. Deep-fry until golden brown as directed on page 29; set aside to drain on paper towels.

Cut fish fillet into ¼-inch-thick slices and carefully butterfly. Bring chicken broth to a boil, skimming fat if necessary. Add SEASONINGS and keep hot.

To assemble, place lettuce in a large serving bowl or tureen. Sprinkle with ginger and onion. Layer fried won-ton wrappers on top. Arrange fish decoratively in a circular pattern on top and sprinkle with sesame seeds and peanuts.

To serve, bring serving bowl to the table. Carefully, oh so carefully, pour piping hot broth over all.

• *Notes* •

1. Remember, the broth must be piping hot when poured in order to cook the raw fish.

2. If you want to simplify the fancy cutting technique for the fish, just slice the fillet into ⅛-inch-thick slices.

Delicate ingredients of fish blossom soup—lettuce, ginger, onion, fried won-ton wrappers, peanuts, and paper-thin slices of fish—await a final touch of steaming chicken broth to be poured over all. Displayed in an antique bowl with lotus famille rose design.

Won-ton Soup *Pictured below*

Without question, this is the most requested Chinese soup in America. In China it is served as an afternoon snack or for a late night supper, but seldom as a soup for dinner.

Makes: 6 servings
Cooking time: 30 minutes

FILLING
- ½ pound lean ground pork
- 1 green onion (including top), minced
- 1 tablespoon dry sherry
- 1 teaspoon sesame oil
- ½ teaspoon sugar
- ¼ teaspoon salt
- Pinch white pepper

- 1½ quarts Rich Chicken Broth (page 52), or chicken bouillon

- 2 dozen won-ton wrappers
- Beaten egg
- 1½ quarts water

- Dash sesame oil
- Chopped green onion

Optional toppings:
sliced barbecued pork, boiled prawns, snow peas, black mushrooms, sliced water chestnuts, or bite-size pieces of Chinese cabbage or fresh spinach

Combine FILLING ingredients; mix well and set aside.

Pour chicken broth in pan to reheat; skim off any fat and season with salt and pepper, if necessary. Cover and simmer over very low heat until ready to serve.

To assemble, spoon about 1 teaspoon filling in center of won-ton wrapper, brush edge with beaten egg, and fold as illustrated on page 29.

To cook, bring water to a boil and drop in won-tons. When water begins to boil, add another 1 cup water to reduce the temperature. When water reaches second boil (about 3 minutes) and won-tons start to float, remove them with a strainer and transfer to a large soup bowl or tureen.

To serve, pour hot chicken broth over won-ton; sprinkle with sesame oil and chopped onion. Garnish with your favorite topping.

• *Notes* •

1. Don't overcook won-tons or the noodle quality and texture will be lost. Don't allow water to come to a rolling boil because this might cause wrappers to break.

2. Won-ton may be cooked ahead of time. Drain well and mix with 1 tablespoon oil until serving, or cover with cold water and refrigerate.

Ginger Clam Soup   *Pictured on page 50, 214*

This simple, elegant soup has a peppery bite from white pepper and ginger. It may make you feel healthier as well: ginger is served for its medicinal qualities in China, and the Chinese believe that "some ginger a day keeps the doctor away."

Makes: 4 servings
Cooking time: 10 minutes

1½ pounds live Manila clams, scrubbed and rinsed
1 quart water

1 quart clear chicken broth (see Notes)
2 thumb-size knobs of fresh ginger, peeled and julienned

SEASONINGS

1 teaspoon salt (to taste)
1 teaspoon Shao Hsing wine
1 or 2 pinches white pepper (to taste)

2 sprigs Chinese parsley (cilantro), finely chopped

To parboil, bring water to a boil in a saucepan. Add clams and boil for 1 minute until clams begin to open. Immediately remove clams to a bowl as they open until all clams are open. Drain well. Discard unopened clams. Discard water.

To boil, bring broth to a boil in a saucepan. Add ginger and simmer 1 minute. Add clams and SEASONINGS. Bring to a low boil and adjust seasonings. The taste should be gingery with some bite from the white pepper. Immediately remove from heat; do not overcook clams.

To serve, divide clams among four soup bowls. Distribute ginger into each bowl. Sprinkle with Chinese parsley and serve.

• *Notes* •

1. It is important to get the flavor of this soup right. It should have the taste of fresh ginger and white pepper, yet allow the essence of delicate fresh clams to come through. The saltiness of the soup depends on the saltiness of the broth and the clams, so adjust the salt accordingly. Be sure to use very fresh, tender young ginger for the soup.

2. When shopping for clams, choose ones that are tightly closed; that indicates they are alive. Less fresh clams are usually slightly open and do not respond by closing when touched or squeezed.

3. You can clarify chicken broth by straining it through cheesecloth or a fine mesh strainer.

4. For presentation, discard any empty shells before serving the soup.

POULTRY

In China, poultry is purchased alive and killed by the vendor or by the cook later at home. This tradition guarantees freshness—the first shrewd step toward serving a good meal.

When examining fresh poultry in China, one would touch the breast to determine whether the fowl is plump or bony, to estimate the overall weight, and to judge its age—whether premature or overgrown.

In the United States, most markets sell refrigerated chicken. Choosing the freshest is difficult; however, try to select a chicken with a yellower color to its skin, as this kind tends to be tastier. Since there are different types of chicken to choose from, do not let size affect your buying, as that does not guarantee tenderness.

Here are a few guidelines: Fryers or broilers, usually weighing 2 to 3 pounds, are good for braising, barbecuing, or deep-frying; roasters, 3 pounds and up, are chickens generally used in restaurants. They are tender and tasty and excellent for making broth. And, because they have more meat, they are the ideal choice when boned chicken is called for.

Poultry is prepared in thousands of scrumptious ways in Chinese cuisine. Minced Chicken in Lettuce Cups (page 71) offers an intriguing assortment of flavors and textures.

Since most recipes in this cookbook specify boned chicken, your best buy is a roaster even though it is more expensive. Roasters weighing 5 pounds will yield about 3 pounds of bones and 2 pounds of meat while a fryer (about 3 pounds) will produce only 1 pound of meat.

Ducks found in American markets are frozen, and while they are quite adequate, a fresh duck is far superior. If you live near a metropolitan city in which there is a Chinatown, a trip to a Chinese butcher is well worth the trouble. There is no easy way to tell how fat a frozen duck is, but when selecting among fresh ducks, look for the plumpest candidate with the least amount of fat.

Poultry seems to make an appearance in virtually every Chinese meal. There are many ways it may be cooked and it can assume a great variety of textures and tastes, from light and velvety to bold and spicy. Cooking time can run the gamut, too, and on days when time is of the essence, quick, stir-fry dishes will allow you to serve a tempting meal in less than 30 minutes. Working people who attend my cooking classes tell me that they have found chicken breasts "on standby" in their refrigerator or freezer to be an essential ingredient for quickly prepared meals—slice or dice, stir-fry, and dinner is virtually ready.

Chicken In Phoenix Nest

The Phoenix, which represents beauty and grace, is properly remembered in the presentation of this dish. Cubes of plump chicken nestle in a lacy basket made of shredded potatoes. Green pepper, slices of carrot, and delicate quail eggs are a colorful and surprising addition.

Makes: 4 to 6 servings
Cooking time: 30 minutes

- 1 large russet potato
  Pinch salt
- 1 broiler-fryer chicken
  (about 2½ lbs.), boned, skinned, and cut into bite-size pieces

MARINADE

- 2 teaspoons light or regular soy sauce
- 2 teaspoons dry sherry
- 1 egg white
- 1 tablespoon cornstarch
- 1 tablespoon vegetable oil

- ½ teaspoon cornstarch

  Vegetable oil, for deep-frying

- 2 green onions (white part), finely chopped
- 1 clove garlic, sliced

SAUCE

- 2 tablespoons soy sauce
- 2 tablespoons Hoisin sauce
- 1 tablespoon dry sherry

VEGETABLES

- 1 green pepper, seeded and cut into 1-inch squares
- ¼ white onion, cut into 1-inch squares
- 6 thin slices carrot

  Dash sesame oil
- 5 or 6 quail eggs
  Shredded lettuce or bok choy

- 2 medium-size wire strainers

Peel potato and shred; place in a bowl of water, add salt and let stand until ready to use.

Combine chicken with MARINADE ingredients in the order listed and let stand for 10 minutes; set aside.

Drain potatoes thoroughly and toss with the ½ teaspoon cornstarch. Heat 2 quarts oil in a wok to 350°.

To shape, dip the 2 identical strainers into the oil to prevent sticking. Distribute half the potatoes evenly around the sides and bottom of one strainer. Press the other strainer down into the potato-lined one.

To deep-fry, holding the strainers tightly together, carefully lower them into the oil and rotate so that oil touches all the sides. Deep-fry for 3 to 4 minutes, basting if necessary, until potato nest becomes slightly brown. Remove from oil, gently separate strainers and tap nest out onto a paper towel to drain. Repeat, using remaining potatoes.

To oil-blanch, remove 1 quart oil (reserve for future use) and heat remaining oil to 300°. Add chicken, stirring to separate, and blanch for 2 to 3 minutes. Remove and drain.

Combine SAUCE ingredients and set aside.

To stir-fry, remove all but 3 tablespoons oil from the wok and when hot, add onion and garlic. Stir-fry until fragrant and then add VEGETABLES and chicken. Cook for 1 minute; stir in SAUCE. Continue cooking and stirring for 1 minute longer, then stir in sesame oil and drained quail eggs.

To serve, position potato nests on top of platter lined with lettuce. Fill each nest with half the chicken mixture, carefully keeping quail egg on top.

Lemon Chicken

I offer you another one of my four-star dishes. Breast of chicken, lightly coated with batter and deep-fried, is topped with a tangy lemon sauce that's so refreshing.

Makes: 6 servings
Cooking time: 45 minutes

3 whole chicken breasts, split, boned, and skinned

MARINADE

¼ cup water
1 tablespoon dry sherry
¼ teaspoon garlic powder
¼ teaspoon salt
Pinch Chinese five-spice

BATTER

½ cup flour
1 cup cornstarch
¼ teaspoon baking powder
1 cup water
1 teaspoon vegetable oil

LEMON SAUCE

1 lemon
1 cup water
½ cup Rose's Lime Juice
¾ cup sugar
¼ teaspoons salt
2 drops yellow food coloring (optional)

Cornstarch
Vegetable oil, for deep-frying

Cornstarch paste
1 tablespoon vegetable oil

1 cup shredded lettuce
Lemon slices
Maraschino cherries, halved

Lightly score both sides of chicken breasts making a crisscross pattern. Combine MARINADE ingredients with chicken; let stand for 10 minutes.

In a bowl, place BATTER ingredients except oil. Using a whisk, beat continuously until the consistency of heavy cream is reached. Stir in oil, mix well, and let stand for 20 minutes.

Cut lemon in fourths; squeeze juice (discarding seeds) into a saucepan, dropping lemon into pan as well. Stir in remaining SAUCE ingredients, bring to a boil, remove and set aside.

To deep-fry, remove chicken from marinade and lightly coat with cornstarch. Heat 4 cups of oil in a wok (or electric deep-fat fryer) to 275° to 300°. Coat chicken in batter, draining off excess. Lower into wok by sliding pieces down the sides; deep-fry for 3 to 4 minutes (about 80% done) until a crust is formed. Remove and drain. (The above procedure may be done in advance.)

Reheat lemon sauce; stir in 2 to 3 tablespoons cornstarch paste and cook until thickened. Stir in 1 tablespoon oil; keep warm.

To deep-fry again, raise oil temperature in wok to 350°, discarding any pieces of batter from the first frying. Add chicken, all at once, and cook for 3 to 4 minutes until golden brown. Remove and drain.

To serve, place lettuce on a large serving platter. Cut chicken into 4 pieces crosswise and place on lettuce bed. Spoon sauce over chicken and garnish with lemon slices and cherries. Offer any extra sauce at the table.

• Notes •

1. Because the chicken should be crunchy on the outside yet juicy and tender on the inside, we've developed a "double-frying" process. The first frying, when the oil temperature is lower, actually cooks the chicken and causes a crust to form on the outside. The second frying at a higher temperature is what produces that special crunchy crust.

2. The lemon sauce should have a sharp, tangy taste and be the consistency of syrup.

3. I always tell my students to double the recipe for lemon sauce; it stores beautifully in the refrigerator for several months.

General's Spicy Hot Chicken

General Chua, a famous Chinese general from the Hunan Province, is reported to have concocted this dish over 100 years. It's hot spicy, and quite tempting. You'll probably enjoy it as much as he did!

Makes: 6 servings
Cooking time: 10 minutes

1 whole chicken breast, split, boned and skinned

MARINADE

1 tablespoon soy sauce
1 teaspoon cornstarch

SAUCE

1 tablespoon white vinegar
1 tablespoon soy sauce
1 tablespoon dry sherry
½ teaspoon sugar
1 teaspoon cornstarch paste

Vegetable oil, for blanching

1 to 2 fresh red or green jalapeños, diced with seeds (to taste)

SEASONINGS

1 green onion (white part), chopped
½ teaspoon minced fresh ginger
1 clove garlic, minced or pressed

2 teaspoons sesame oil

Pound chicken slightly with a mallet to tenderize; then cut into ³/₄-by ³/₄-inch pieces. Combine MARINADE ingredients with chicken in the order listed; set aside.

Combine SAUCE ingredients thoroughly; set aside.

To oil-blanch, set wok over high heat for about 1 minute. Add 2 cups oil and heat to 350°. Add chicken and blanch for 3 or 4 minutes until golden brown. Remove and drain.

To stir-fry, remove all but 2 tablespoons oil from wok. Reheat, swirling pan to coat sides. Add jalapeños and seeds; stir-fry for 10 to 15 seconds until fragrant. Return chicken and add SEASONINGS, stir-frying for another 30 seconds. Add SAUCE and stir until thickened. Stir in sesame oil and serve.

• Notes •

1. Traditionally this dish is made with dried whole red chili pods, broken in half with the seeds included. You can use three dried chili pods instead of the fresh jalapeños. Stir-fry chilies in 2 tablespoons oil for 20 to 30 seconds until browned before adding chicken.

2. Including the seeds of the fresh jalapeños will make this dish fiery. For a milder dish, remove and discard the seeds.

Minced Chicken in Lettuce Cups *Pictured on page 66*

Classic and simple to prepare, this beautiful dish is easy to serve, healthy and delicious. Although this is usually served in lettuce cups, we suggest that you try serving it in hearts of romaine lettuce leaves or Belgian endive for an eye-catching presentation.

Makes: 6 to 8 servings
Cooking time: 15 minutes

4 or 5 dried black mushrooms

1 whole chicken breast, split, boned and skinned

MARINADE

Pinch white pepper
1 egg white
½ teaspoon cornstarch
1 tablespoon vegetable oil

SAUCE

1 tablespoon dry sherry
1 tablespoon oyster sauce
3 tablespoons Hoisin sauce
¼ teaspoon salt

1 head iceberg lettuce (or 3 to 4 heads Belgium endive or hearts of romaine, leaves separated)

Vegetable oil, for deep-frying
1 ounce rice sticks, separated into smaller amounts

1 green onion (white part), chopped
½ cup coarsely chopped bamboo shoots
2 water chestnuts, coarsely chopped
2 tablespoons coarsely chopped red bell pepper

2 tablespoons toasted pinenuts or crushed peanuts

Soak mushrooms in warm water for 20 minutes; remove, drain, and dice.

Mince chicken and combine with MARINADE ingredients in the order listed; let stand for 10 minutes. Combine SAUCE ingredients in a bowl.

Cut 1 inch off the core end of lettuce head. Peel off large leaves and trim with scissors or pinking shears to make circles about 4 or 5 inches in diameter.

To deep-fry, heat 2 cups oil in a wok to 350°. Fry rice sticks in batches, a small amount at a time, for a few seconds until puffed, but still white. Remove immediately, drain well.

To stir-fry, remove all oil from wok except 3 tablespoons. Reheat oil until hot. Add chicken and stir-fry for 1 to 2 minutes until opaque. Add green onion, bamboo shoots, mushrooms, water chestnuts and red bell pepper, and stir for 30 to 45 seconds. Add SAUCE, tossing vigorously to coat thoroughly.

To serve, mound chicken mixture in the center of serving platter. Sprinkle pinenuts over the mound. Sprinkle rice sticks around the edge of the mound. Place lettuce cups around outside edge of mound or on a separate plate. Spoon 2 tablespoons of chicken mixture into each leaf. Sprinkle some rice sticks on top. Eat out-of-hand.

Alternative Serving Method: To serve at a buffet or cocktail party, spoon chicken mixture into each leaf, sprinkle with pinenuts and rice sticks and arrange decoratively on a platter or tray for each person to serve himself.

• Notes •

1. Vegetarian version: Omit the chicken and increase the amount of bamboo shoots to 1 cup and water chestnuts to ¼ cup. You can also add ½ cup coarsely chopped celery, squash or fresh mushrooms to the mixture. For a spicy version, add 1 seeded, thinly sliced jalapeño with the vegetables.

2. Rice sticks will expand greatly in size when deep-fried; cook only a little at a time. Do not brown.

Chef Chu's Famous Chicken Salad

Pictured on facing page

This dish is quick, healthy, simple and delicious. To maintain its light fluffy quality, we toss the ingredients at the last minute so it's nice and crisp. Our light mustard and sesame oil dressing, along with a dash of Five-spice Salt, give it a bit of a bite!

Makes: 12 servings
Cooking time: 25 to 30 minutes

1 pound cooked chicken, (about 2 cups)

2 cups vegetable oil
2 ounces rice sticks, pulled apart into smaller pieces

HOT MUSTARD PASTE

2 teaspoons Colman's Hot Mustard Powder
2 teaspoons water
1 tablespoon sesame oil

Half-head iceberg lettuce, shredded ¼-inch
½ cup julienned carrots
10 to 12 sprigs Chinese parsley (cilantro) with stems, coarsely chopped
½ teaspoon Five-spice Salt (page 212)

¼ cup crushed roasted peanuts
1 tablespoon toasted sesame seeds
4 Chinese parsley (cilantro) sprigs

Hand-shred the chicken meat by pulling it apart in strands along the grain or julienne it with a knife. Set aside.

To deep-fry, heat vegetable oil in a wok to 375°. Add rice sticks in small batches; deep-fry each batch a few seconds until puffy but still white. (Do not brown.) Remove and drain on paper towels.

To make HOT MUSTARD PASTE, stir mustard and water together in a small bowl to make a paste. Stir in sesame oil until paste becomes smooth and shiny.

To assemble, the secret to the success of this salad is how it is assembled. Place lettuce, carrot and chopped Chinese parsley in a large salad bowl. Sprinkle Five-spice Salt evenly over lettuce mixture. Toss well to distribute salt evenly. Rub HOT MUSTARD PASTE around lower sides of bowl. Add chicken, peanuts and sesame seeds evenly over lettuce. Toss well to distribute HOT MUSTARD PASTE evenly throughout salad. Adjust taste. Add three-quarters of the rice sticks last; toss lightly to distribute evenly. Reserve remaining rice sticks for garnish.

To serve, mound salad on individual salad plates. Sprinkle remaining rice sticks over the top. Sprinkle with peanuts and sesame seeds. Garnish with a sprig of Chinese parsley.

• Notes •

1. You may use leftover cooked chicken (fried, barbecued, rotisserie, steamed, smoked or pan-fried) or duck for a different flavor. Slightly warm the chicken or duck, or serve at room temperature, for richer flavor.

2. Add the crisp poultry skin, julienned, to add texture and flavor to the salad.

3. Five-spice Salt is added to the lettuce first to distribute it evenly. If added when the HOT MUSTARD PASTE is tossed in, it can stick to the mustard and have an unpleasant taste. Also, if added too early, it can wilt the lettuce.

4. Some customers enjoy sprinkling a little of Chef Chu's Garlic Dipping Sauce (page 212) over each individual serving for a different flavor sensation.

Snow White Chicken

Plump chicken breasts are sliced paper thin and then lightly marinated before being stir-fried with snow peas and black mushrooms. I recommend it to my customers who prefer a mildly-flavored chicken dish.

Makes: 6 servings
Cooking time: 10 minutes

4 dried black mushrooms

1 whole chicken breast, split, boned, and skinned

MARINADE

¼ teaspoon salt
Pinch white pepper
3 tablespoons water
1 egg white
1 tablespoon cornstarch
1 tablespoon vegetable oil

SAUCE

1 green onion (white part), finely chopped
¼ teaspoon minced fresh ginger
1 cup Rich Chicken Broth (page 52), or chicken bouillon
1½ tablespoons dry sherry
¼ teaspoon salt
Pinch white pepper
¼ teaspoon sugar
1 tablespoon cornstarch paste

Vegetable oil, for blanching
5 or 6 snow peas, ends trimmed and cut in half

Soak mushrooms in warm water for 20 minutes; drain, remove stems, and cut in half.

Partially freeze chicken breast, then slice paper thin (about ⅛-inch thick). Combine MARINADE ingredients with chicken in the order listed. Let stand for about 10 minutes.

Combine SAUCE ingredients thoroughly; set aside.

To oil-blanch, set wok over high heat for about 1 minute. Add 4 cups oil and heat to 300°. Add chicken, stirring to separate pieces. Turn off heat and add snow peas and mushrooms; blanch for about 15 seconds, then remove and drain.

To stir-fry, remove all but 2 tablespoons oil from wok. Turn heat on high, add sauce and cook until thickened. Add chicken mixture, lightly stir-fry to coat thoroughly for about 30 seconds.

• *Note* •

A good rich chicken broth is required for this dish. If you don't have any Rich Chicken Broth (page 52), dissolve an additional bouillon cube in the broth you're using to increase the flavor.

Kung Pao Chicken

As the story goes, the chef of a provincial viceroy, a *kung pao,* made a mistake whilst cooking dinner—he overbrowned the chili in the hot oil before adding the chicken; however, in so doing, he created an aroma which was spicy and smoky. To his good fortune, his viceroy loved it, and both the dish and the story became widespread. The number of dried chili pods in this recipe indicates that this dish is fiery hot.

Makes: 8 servings
Cooking time: 15 minutes

1 whole chicken breast, split, boned, and skinned

MARINADE
2 teaspoons soy sauce
2 teaspoons dry sherry
1 teaspoon cornstarch
1 tablespoon vegetable oil

Vegetable oil, for blanching

SEASONINGS
3 tablespoons soy sauce
1 tablespoon dry sherry
2 tablespoons red rice vinegar
1 teaspoon sugar
½ teaspoon cornstarch paste

10 dried red chili pods

VEGETABLES
6 to 8 water chestnuts, cut in fourths
¼ cup diced bamboo shoots
2 green onions (white part), cut in ½-inch pieces
1 clove garlic, minced or pressed

¼ teaspoon sesame oil
1 teaspoon hot chili oil
¼ cup roasted peanuts

Bone chicken, remove skin and cut meat into ¾-inch cubes. Combine with MARINADE ingredients in the order listed; set aside.

To oil-blanch, set wok over high heat for about 1 minute. Add 2 cups oil and heat to 300°. Add chicken, stirring to separate pieces. Remove and drain.

Combine SEASONINGS thoroughly; set aside.

To stir-fry, remove all but 2 tablespoons oil from wok. Reheat, swirling pan to coat sides. Add chili pods, breaking only one in half. Stir for about 45 seconds or until browned (but not burned). Return chicken and cook for 1 to 2 minutes until browned. Add VEGETABLES, stir-frying for 1 minute. Add SEASONINGS, mixing thoroughly, and cook until thickened. Sprinkle with sesame and hot chili oils and finally with roasted peanuts to serve.

• *Note* •

Chili seeds, not pods, determine just how hot a dish will be. I suggest breaking open only one the first time; if you want it hotter, open more next time.

After applying skill and patience to the preparation of Peking Duck, take some care with the presentation, too. The aim is to remove the bones, then reassemble the skin and meat to recreate the duck's original shape. 1), 2) Carve off the duck's legs and wings, and then 3) remove skin from the back and 4) breasts. 5) Cut meat and place bite-size pieces on serving platter; cover with skin and 6) arrange legs, wings, and head to create original shape. Serve with steamed Mandarin pancakes, Peking sauce, and onion slivers. (A dish containing shredded pieces of duck and celery—for extra nibbling—is in the foreground.)

Classic Peking Duck   *Pictured on page 76*

This truly grand duck will challenge the best of cooks but the secret is patience; pay careful attention to this recipe, and results will earn you the chef's hat.

Makes: 8 servings
Cooking time: 2 hours

1 fresh duck (5 lbs. or larger), cleaned with head attached
2 quarts water
½ teaspoon baking soda

COATING

1 quart water
1 tablespoon maltose or honey

12 to 18 Mandarin Pancakes (page 187)
8 Onion Brushes (page 217)

PEKING SAUCE

2 tablespoons Hoisin sauce
¼ teaspoon sesame oil
¼ teaspoon sugar

This first procedure is an optional but authentic step in making Peking duck.

Seal tail opening with a skewer. Using a pump, force air in between skin and meat by inserting it at neck opening. When inflated, seal off at neck with a piece of string. (The air will escape naturally during cooking.)

To water-blanch, bring water and soda to a boil. Drop in duck, ladling water over it as necessary, and blanch for about 30 seconds. Remove duck, discarding water.

To coat, bring water and maltose to a boil in a wok. Holding duck over wok, ladle coating syrup evenly all over surface; repeat about 6 times.

Hang duck in a cool place (preferably near a fan) with circulating air for at least 4 hours or longer until skin is dry to the touch.

To roast, preheat oven to 400°. Place duck, breast side up, on a V-shaped rack in a roasting pan. Cover loosely with a tent of aluminum foil (avoid touching skin), and roast for 30 minutes.

Meanwhile, make pancakes as directed on page 187; set aside to be steamed just before serving. Carve onion brushes as directed on page 217; set aside.

Combine SAUCE ingredients and set aside

To continue roasting, turn duck over on rack, cover with foil, and continue roasting for 30 minutes longer. Then turn duck over, breast side up, and remove foil. Roast for 5 to 10 minutes more or until golden brown (watch carefully to prevent burning).

Place pancakes wrapped in damp towel inside steamer. Cover and steam for about 3 minutes; keep warm.

To carve, transfer duck to a cutting board. Carefully, remove skin in large pieces; cut meat from carcass into bite-size pieces and arrange on serving platter. Cover with skin pieces and position wings and legs properly, recreating its original shape (see page 77). Garnish plate with onion brushes.

To serve, brush warm pancake with Peking Sauce, add onion and a few pieces of duck and skin. Roll up and eat out of hand.

Yuen Pao Duck

This succulent whole duck is impressive served with a treasure of golden crispy fried won-tons called *yuen pao*, which resemble the ancient Chinese gold nuggets that symbolize wealth and prosperity.

Makes: 10 to 12 servings
Cooking time: 1¾ to 2 hours

1 whole duck (4 to 5 lbs.) (with head, optional), wing tips removed

MARINADE

½ cup soy sauce
2 tablespoons sugar
2 tablespoons Shao Hsing wine
5 thick ginger slices, crushed
2 green onions, crushed
3 whole star anise
1 quart vegetable oil
Fried Won-ton (page 29), assemble recipe, but do not fry

SEASONINGS

2 green onions, cut into 2-inch lengths
10 fancy-cut ginger slices, about 2 inches long
10 cloud ears soaked 30 minutes, drained, tough parts removed
3 tablespoons cornstarch paste
1 tablespoon sesame oil
4 to 6 leaves curly lettuce or sliced cucumbers

To serve, place half of the won-tons in the center of serving platter. Reform duck shape, breast-side up, covering won-tons underneath. Ladle all the sauce over duck to glaze evenly. Place remaining fried won-tons around the edges of the platter. Duck should be soft enough to serve with a spoon. The sauce-drenched lettuce is delicious with the duck.

Split duck along backbone to butterfly; leave breast side intact. Turn duck, skin side up, on chopping board. Break breast and leg bones with the back of a cleaver without breaking the skin. Combine MARINADE ingredients in a large bowl. Add duck and turn to coat all sides. Marinate duck for at least 30 minutes. (Or marinate duck for a few hours or overnight, covered, in the refrigerator. Turn duck a few times during marinating).

To deep-fry, heat 1 quart oil to 365° in a large wok. Lift duck from MARINADE, leaving solids in MARINADE. Reserve MARINADE. Carefully place duck in oil, breast side down. Deep-fry duck for 5 minutes to give the skin color, or until golden brown. (Press duck edges into the oil to brown evenly.) Remove duck and place breast-side down, in a heat proof 8- to 10-inch mixing bowl that will fit inside a steamer. Pour reserved MARINADE and solids over the duck. Reserve oil.

To steam, place bowl on a steamer rack over boiling water. Cover and steam for 1½ hours until duck is very tender but still holds its shape. Replenish steamer water, if needed.

To assemble, prepare won-ton recipe to make *yuen pao* while duck is steaming, making 24 total. (To prepare hours ahead, place raw won-tons apart on a tray covered with plastic wrap. Refrigerate until ready to deep-fry.)

Line the edge of a large rimmed serving platter with curly lettuce leaves, stems pointing inward. Set aside.

When duck is done steaming, remove from steamer. Pour duck liquid through a strainer into another bowl. Remove and discard solids. Remove duck fat from liquid and discard. Reserve liquid for making sauce.

To deep-fry won-tons, reheat oil to 350°. Deep-fry won-tons in 2 batches until golden brown; drain well.

To stir-fry, remove all but 1 tablespoon oil from wok. Reheat oil until hot. Add SEASONINGS, stir for 30 seconds. Add reserved duck liquid. Boil for 1 minute. Adjust seasonings. Thicken with enough cornstarch paste to make a medium-light sauce. Stir in sesame oil.

What better way to put a spark in the holidays than to prepare your roast turkey with a Chinese twist? Eight-Treasure Stuffing (page 81) is a fresh take on traditional bread stuffing using Chinese sausage, bamboo shoots, fresh mushrooms, green onion and celery. Accompany it with vibrantly hued Snow Peas With Water Chestnuts (page 146) or Mixed Chinese Vegetables (page 188, not shown), and end with palate-pleasing Pineapple Crescents (page 188) for a truly memorable meal.

Turkey With Eight Treasure Stuffing

Pictured on facing page

At holiday time, try this Chinese stuffing. It is easy to make and a surprise to serve. To depart from the ordinary completely, let your next festive occasion follow a Chinese turkey dinner menu commencing with Won-ton Soup and concluding with Pineapple Crescents.

Makes: 16 to 20 servings
Cooking time: 5 hours

1 turkey (14 to 15 lbs.)

MARINADE
4 green onions
1 thumb-size chunk fresh ginger, smashed
3 tablespoons dry sherry
1 tablespoon roasted Szechuan peppercorns
2 tablespoons salt

1½ cups sweet rice

STUFFING
4 dried black mushrooms
2 tablespoons dried shrimp
1 small piece (about 2 ounces) Virginia ham or Chinese sausage, chopped (optional)
5 tablespoons dried red dates, seeds removed and chopped
2 tablespoons raisins
1 green onion (white part), chopped
2 preserved candied kumquats, chopped
10 canned gingko nuts, chopped

2 tablespoons vegetable oil

SEASONINGS
2 tablespoons soy sauce
½ teaspoon sugar
1 teaspoon salt
¼ teaspoon white pepper

COATING
3 tablespoons honey
½ cup hot water

Curly endive
Plum sauce (purchased)

Remove giblets and set aside; reserve other innards for other uses. Combine MARINADE ingredients and rub on turkey, inside and out. Let stand for 2 hours (or overnight in refrigerator).

Soak rice in warm water for 1 hour. Then line the inside of a steamer with wet cheesecloth. Place rice on cheesecloth, cover, and steam over boiling water for 25 minutes. Remove and set aside.

Soak mushrooms in warm water for 30 minutes; drain, remove stems, and chop. Soak shrimp in warm water for 30 minutes; remove, drain, and chop.

In a large bowl, combine STUFFING ingredients and cooked rice; add oil and SEASONINGS and mix well.

To stuff, remove seasonings clinging to turkey. Spoon stuffing into turkey. (Take care not to overstuff and allow room for expansion.) Close openings with skewers.

Combine COATING ingredients and brush evenly over turkey. Let stand for 10 minutes.

To roast, preheat oven to 350°. Place turkey, breast side up, on V-shaped rack in roasting pan. Arrange giblets around edges of pan. Cover with a tent of aluminum foil. Allowing 20 minutes per pound, roast turkey brushing occasionally with honey glaze until juices run clear when thigh is pierced. Remove cooked giblets and chop; set aside. Remove foil and increase temperature to 375° to 400° to brown just before serving, if desired.

To serve, make favorite gravy and add chopped giblets; keep warm. Border a large serving platter with curly endive. Slice turkey and arrange on platter. Remove stuffing and mound into center. Offer plum sauce.

Crisp Spicy Duck

The spicy marinade permeates and flavors the meat to make this crispy delicacy a mouth-watering family dish. Serve with steamed buns, slivers of onion, and spicy Hoisin sauce.

Makes: 6 to 8 servings
Cooking time: 75 minutes

1 large fresh duck (4½ to 5 lbs.), cleaned

MARINADE

2 green onions, cut in half
2 thumb-size chunks fresh ginger, crushed
1 tablespoon Szechuan peppercorns
3 tablespoons dry sherry
3 tablespoons salt

2 tablespoons soy sauce
3 tablespoons flour

1 dozen Butterfly Steamed Buns (page 176)

Vegetable oil, for deep-frying

Slivers of green onion
Hoisin sauce

Rub duck inside and out with MARINADE ingredients; let stand for 8 hours or overnight in refrigerator.

To steam, place duck on rack in steamer. Cover and steam over boiling water for 1 hour. Remove, discarding spices clinging to duck. Brush duck with soy sauce and dust with flour, shaking off excess. (The above procedure may be done in advance.)

Prepare buns following directions on page 176; set aside until ready for steaming.

To deep-fry, heat 4 cups oil in wok (or electric deep-fat fryer) to 350°. Fry duck for 10 to 12 minutes, turning occasionally with a spatula to prevent skin from sticking to the bottom. Remove when duck is golden brown.

Meanwhile, place buns on rack in bamboo steamer. Cover and steam over boiling water for about 5 minutes.

To serve, cut duck into major parts, then slice ½-inch thick including the bone. Reassemble on platter recreating the original shape as illustrated on page 85. Offer steamed buns, onion slivers, and Hoisin sauce at the table.

• *Note* •

If you find it more comfortable, cut the duck in half before the deep-frying process.

Sautéed Ginger Duck

Unlike most Chinese duck recipes calling for roasting, steaming, or braising, this one specifies sautéeing. It's one of my favorites because preparing duck this way creates such a unique texture and flavor.

Makes: 8 servings
Cooking time: 10 minutes

1 fresh duck (3 to 4 lbs.), cleaned

MARINADE
- 1 teaspoon soy sauce
  Pinch white pepper
- 1 egg white
- 1 teaspoon cornstarch
- 1 tablespoon vegetable oil

SAUCE
- 2 teaspoons soy sauce
- 1 teaspoon dry sherry
- 1 teaspoon white vinegar
- ½ teaspoon cornstarch paste
- ¼ teaspoon sugar
- ¼ teaspoon sesame oil

  Vegetable oil, for blanching

VEGETABLES
- 20 thin slices fresh ginger
- 10 snow peas, ends trimmed and diagonally cut in half
- 10 to 15 canned straw mushrooms
- 1 green onion (white part), diagonally sliced ½-inch thick
- 2 cloves garlic, sliced

  Pinch salt

Bone duck; cutting with the grain, slice meat about ⅛-inch thick.

Combine MARINADE ingredients with duck in the order listed, mixing well. Let stand for 10 minutes.

Combine SAUCE ingredients thoroughly; set aside.

To oil-blanch, heat wok over high heat for about 1 minute. Add 2 cups oil and heat to 350°. Add duck slices, stirring for 15 seconds to separate. Remove and drain.

To stir-fry, remove all but 3 tablespoons oil from wok. Reheat, swirling pan to coat sides. Add VEGETABLES and salt; stir-fry for about 15 seconds and then return duck to wok. Quickly stir in sauce, tossing to coat duck pieces thoroughly. Transfer to a serving platter.

• Notes •

1. It's easier to slice meat—especially when the recipe calls for paper-thin slices—if you partially freeze it first.

2. You may have noticed that we call for a higher blanching temperature in this recipe. It's needed to quickly seal in the juices, thus creating a more tender texture in the duck.

Tea-smoked Duck

Tea-smoked duck, often served in Szechuan-style Chinese restaurants, takes a little more time to prepare but it's worth it. The meat is tender and juicy with a hint of smoky flavor that's irresistible.

Makes: 8 servings
Cooking time: 1½ hours

1   large fresh duck (4½ to 5 lbs.), cleaned

MARINADE

2   green onions, cut in half
2   thumb-size chunks fresh ginger, crushed
5   star anise seeds, broken
3   tablespoons dry sherry
1   tablespoon Szechuan peppercorns
3   tablespoons salt
¼   teaspoon curing salt (optional)

1   dozen Butterfly Steamed Buns (page 176)

3   tablespoons black tea leaves
2   tablespoons brown sugar
2   tablespoons rice

Vegetable oil, for deep-frying

Slivers of green onion

Rub duck inside and out with MARINADE ingredients. Let stand for 8 hours or overnight in the refrigerator.

Prepare buns following directions on page 176; set aside until ready for steaming.

To steam, place duck on rack inside steamer. Cover and steam over boiling water for 1 hour. Remove, discarding spices clinging to duck.

To smoke, line a 14-inch wok and its cover with aluminum foil. Sprinkle tea leaves over foil, then sugar and then rice. Place duck, breast side up, on a V-shaped rack in wok. Cover and cook on high heat for 2 minutes. Turn heat off for 5 minutes; then back on for 2 minutes and off again for 5 minutes. (Don't take the lid off during the smoking process.) Remove duck and hang up to cool; discard smoking material. (The above procedure may be done in advance.)

To deep-fry, heat 4 cups oil in wok (or electric deep-fat fryer) to 350°. Fry duck, turning over once, for 10 to 12 minutes or until coffee brown. Watch closely to prevent duck from getting too dark. Remove and drain.

Meanwhile, steam buns in steamer over boiling water for 5 minutes until hot; keep warm.

To serve, cut duck into major parts; then slice ½-inch thick including the bone. Reassemble on platter recreating the original shape (see illustrations on facing page). Offer steamed buns and onion slivers at the table.

• Notes •

1. In some parts of China, cooks prefer wood shavings or pine needles instead of tea leaves for smoking. The type of wood shavings used determines the flavor produced by the fragrance of the smoke.

2. Lining the wok with aluminum foil first prevents the carmelized sugar from sticking to the bottom.

3. If you wish, offer Hoisin sauce as a condiment, too. But go easy—you don't want to overpower the subtle tea-smoked flavor.

Carving a Duck

1) Cut duck in half along backbone. 2) Carefully, remove wings and thigh sections; then 3) separate breasts from back sections. 4) Chop entire back section into bite-size pieces and place in center of platter. Separate legs from thighs and 5) chop thighs into bite-size pieces. Place at one end of platter. 6) Cut breasts into pieces and arrange nicely on top of backbone pieces. Cut legs into pieces and arrange with wings on platter 7) recreating duck's original shape. To serve, 8) open steamed butterfly bun, spread with little sauce, add onion sliver and piece of duck; eat just like a sandwich.

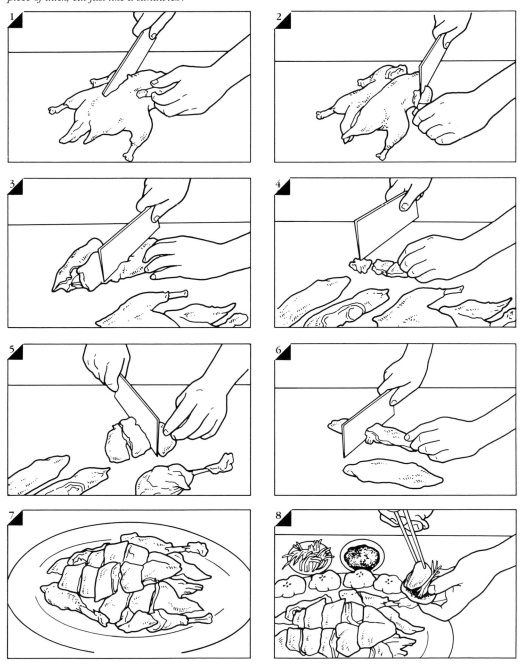

Mandarin Pressed Duck

Crunchy on the outside, tender on the inside, this carefully prepared deboned duck dish was devised by early Chinese cooks in this country for American diners.

Makes: 8 to 10 servings
Cooking time: 2 hours

MASTER SAUCE
- 4 quarts water
- 2 knobs fresh ginger, crushed
- 4 green onions, tied in knots

In a cheesecloth bag put:
- 6 star anise
- 1 teaspoon Szechuan peppercorns
- 1 teaspoon fennel seed
- 2 pieces preserved tangerine peel
- 5 cardamom seeds
- ½ teaspoon whole cloves

- ¾ cup soy sauce
- 4 teaspoons sugar

- 1 fresh duck (4½ to 5 lbs.), cleaned
- 1 tablespoon soy sauce

  Vegetable oil, for blanching

- 2 ounces ground pork
- 4 tablespoons water chestnut starch or cornstarch

- 1 cup Sweet & Sour Sauce (page 213) or canned plum sauce
  Cornstarch paste

  Vegetable oil, for deep-frying

  Shredded lettuce
- 2 tablespoons roasted almonds, crushed

In a deep pot, bring water to a boil; add remaining MASTER SAUCE ingredients including the cheesecloth bag. Reduce heat and simmer for about 30 minutes. Stir in soy sauce and sugar; continue to simmer.

Trim fat around neck and tail of duck; split in half and brush skin with soy sauce.

To oil-blanch, set wok over high heat for about 1 minute. Add 4 cups oil and heat to 350°. Immerse duck in oil (watch out for splattering) and blanch for about 2 minutes or until skin is browned. Remove and drain.

To simmer, place duck in simmering master sauce and continue to simmer for about 45 minutes. Remove (discarding spices that cling to sides) and drain. (Reserve master sauce for other uses.)

To assemble, cut off legs and wings from duck. Peel off skin from breasts without tearing and place right side down on platter. Tear meat off duck, including off legs and wings; finely shred and place in a mixing bowl. Add pork, water chestnut starch or cornstarch, and 4 tablespoons of the master sauce. Spoon mixture out onto both duck skins, pressing down tightly against skin.

To steam, place bowls (or pie tins) filled with duck into steamer. Cover and steam over boiling water for 15 minutes. Remove from steam, pat meat down slightly, and allow to cool. Invert bowls to turn out both duck sections. Cut into wedges like a pie.

In a small saucepan, heat Sweet & Sour sauce and thicken with about 1 tablespoon cornstarch paste; keep warm.

To deep-fry, heat 4 cups oil in a wok (or electric deep-fat fryer) to 350°. Carefully, deep-fry pressed duck wedges, a few at a time, for 6 to 8 minutes or until brown. Remove and drain.

To serve, arrange shredded lettuce on serving platter. Place duck wedges attractively on lettuce, and spoon warm sauce over duck. Garnish with almonds.

Squab Cantonese

Fresh squab goes through two cooking processes to achieve its barbecue-like flavor. After marinating for about 2 hours, it's steamed and then deep-fried. The result is a tender, tasty bird beneath a crisp and golden brown skin.

Makes: 6 to 8 servings
Cooking time: 30 minutes

MARINADE

- 2 green onions, cut in half and crushed to bring out juices
- 1 thumb-size chunk fresh ginger, sliced
- 2 star anise seed, crushed
- 4 tablespoons soy sauce
- 2 tablespoons dry sherry
- ½ teaspoon sugar
- ¼ teaspoon salt

- 2 large squab (1 lb. each), cleaned

  Vegetable oil, for deep-frying

  Shredded lettuce
  Chinese Five-spice Salt
  (page 212)

Combine MARINADE ingredients together; rub squabs inside and out and let stand for 2 hours.

To steam, place squab on plate (or pie tin) inside steamer. Cover and steam over boiling water for 10 minutes. Remove, discarding spices that may be clinging to sides of squab.

To deep-fry, heat 4 cups oil in a wok (or electric deep-fat fryer) to 350°. Fry squabs, one at a time, for about 1 minute. Lift out of oil for 30 seconds, then return to fry for about 1 minute longer or until golden brown.

To serve, cut squabs into 2 sections lengthwise; then cut each section into 3 parts, including the bone. Reassemble on bed of lettuce to recreate original shape. Offer a small dish of five-spice salt for dipping.

• Notes •

1. If you prefer to use quail, you'll need four of them. Remember to cut the steaming time in half.

2. If you use chicken, you'll need one weighing about 2½ pounds.

SEAFOOD

China has more than 8,500 miles of coastline fronting on the Pacific Ocean, with its northernmost region of Shandong embracing the Yellow Sea, with Shanghai and the eastern region facing the East China Sea, and with Canton, an active trading region, boldly exposed to the South China Sea. Two very lengthy rivers, the Yangtze and Yellow, twist and wind through the vast countryside, and thousands of lakes add to the variety of marine life. It is no wonder that this abundance finds its way into many dishes and conversations among Chinese chefs.

The recipes that follow are among the best from the four major regional schools of cooking: Sole Fillets in Wine Sauce from Peking, Prawns in Lobster Sauce from Canton, Spicy Hot Braised Fish from Szechuan, and Crab in Bean Sauce from Shanghai.

American seafood markets offer a great variety of fish. I recommend rock cod and red snapper often because they are easy to handle, good sized, and have a modest number of bones.

When selecting a whole fish, check the eyes to see that they are clear, shiny, and protruding. Gills should be pinkish-red; the body should be firm and shiny. Rub your finger along the fish's body to make sure it bounces back and feels sleek, not sticky. It should have a fish smell, but not a strong one. When selecting fillets of sole, look for those with a shiny glaze.

Prawns generally come fresh-frozen in 5-pound block boxes. If you have a sizeable freezer, this is the most economical way to buy them. When partially thawed, break them into smaller blocks and then refreeze to have them readily available. When buying loose prawns, look for those with a grayish-blue tinge to the shell and a translucent color to the flesh. Do not buy raw prawns already peeled and deveined because chemicals have been added to prolong their shelf life. Prawns that have been cooked and peeled should be light pink in color.

When buying clams, check that their shells are tightly shut; if they are open, even slightly, they are dead and should not be purchased. Put live clams in clear cold water for them to breathe and spew sand trapped inside. Clams should open after blanching in boiling water; discard those that don't!

Crab season is from November to mid-spring, so that is the time to cook crab dishes. Buy them live and prepare them according to the recipes. If you want to offer crab in the off-season, buy them fresh-frozen and cook immediately.

Selecting seafood for freshness and quality is crucial to preparing a delicious, healthful dish. Dungeness Crab With Golden Garlic Crust (page 107) will surprise and delight your guests.

Dragon-whiskered Prawns

This dish is usually served as an appetizer. Chinese like to use whole shrimp because the heads and legs become crunchy and edible, and the feelers look impressive sticking out of the plate.

Makes: 6 to 8 servings
Cooking time: 10 minutes

- 1 pound fresh medium prawns (26 to 30 count) heads and shells on, rinsed and patted dry
- ¾ teaspoon Five-spice Salt, divided (page 212)
- 1 cup cornstarch for dredging
- 3 cups vegetable oil, for deep-frying

SPICES

- ½ medium yellow onion, julienned
- 1 red jalapeño pepper with seeds, julienned (see Note)
- 3 green onions, sliced diagonally
- 1 teaspoon minced garlic
  Curly lettuce leaves

To prepare prawns, use a scissor to trim off the sharp point on the tail and two points near eyes. Leave the long feelers intact. Devein shrimp (see illustration). Rinse and pat dry. Toss prawns with ½ teaspoon Five-spice Salt. Lightly dredge prawns in cornstarch.

Prepare SPICES. Line edges of a platter with lettuce leaves.

To deep-fry, heat 3 cups oil in a wok to 375°. Working in batches, place 6 to 7 prawns in the oil, without moving prawns, for 20 to 30 seconds until a golden crust is formed. Turn once and fry for another 30 seconds. Remove and drain. Skim off sediment and residue from oil between batches.

To stir-fry, remove all oil from the wok, except 2 tablespoons. Reheat oil in wok until hot. Add SPICES and stir-fry for 30 seconds or until onions become translucent. Add prawns and remaining ¼ teaspoon Five-spice Salt. Toss vigorously for 20 seconds until prawns are lightly coated with seasonings.

To serve, transfer prawns to prepared platter.

• *Note* •

If you prefer a less spicy flavor, remove the seeds of the jalapeño before dicing.

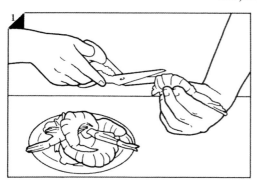

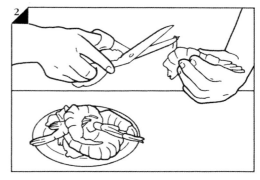

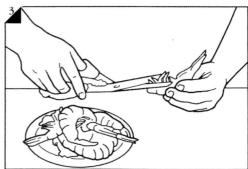

1) Cut along back of prawns with small scissors, leaving shell on. 2) Carefully, lift out black vein and then 3) snip off legs and hard-pointed tips of tail.

Prawns In Lobster Sauce

This isn't as decadent as it sounds! Actually, there isn't any lobster in this Cantonese dish at all. It's just that the color and the taste will fool anyone.

Makes: 6 servings
Cooking time: 10 minutes

1 pound medium-size prawns (26 to 30 count)

MARINADE

Pinch salt
Pinch white pepper
1 egg white
1 teaspoon cornstarch
1 tablespoon vegetable oil

Vegetable oil, for blanching

1 ounce ground pork
1 tablespoon fermented black beans, smashed
1 clove garlic, minced or pressed

VEGETABLES

1 green pepper, cut into ½-inch squares
½ small white onion, cut into ½-inch squares
4 or 5 slices water chestnuts

1 tablespoon dry sherry

SEASONINGS

½ cup chicken broth
¼ teaspoon salt
¼ teaspoon sugar
1 tablespoon soy sauce

Cornstarch paste

2 eggs, lightly beaten
Dash sesame oil

Shell, devein, and rinse prawns. Pat dry and combine with MARINADE ingredients in the order listed; set aside for 10 minutes.

To oil-blanch, set wok over high heat for about 1 minute. Add 3 cups oil and heat to 300°. Add prawns stirring to separate. Blanch for 1 minute; then remove and drain.

To stir-fry, remove all but 3 tablespoons oil from wok. Add pork and fry until separated. Stir in black beans and garlic; cook until fragrant. Add VEGETABLES and sherry, stirring for about 15 seconds. Return prawns and add SEASONINGS. Bring to a boil and thicken with about 2 teaspoons cornstarch paste. Gently stir eggs in one direction and fold into mixture but don't overcook. Add dash sesame oil and remove from heat. Serve immediately.

Empress Prawns

These prawns are velvety and delicate in texture. The dish befits an empress, with its rich traditional Chinese ingredients and colorful vegetables, which sparkle like majestic jewels.

Makes: 6 to 8 servings
Cooking time: 30 to 40 minutes

1 pound jumbo prawns (16 to 20 count), shelled, deveined, rinsed and patted dry

MARINADE
- ¼ teaspoon salt
- Pinch white pepper
- 1 egg white
- 2 teaspoons cornstarch
- 1 tablespoon oil

SAUCE
- 3 tablespoons chicken broth
- 1 green onion (white part) finely chopped
- ½ teaspoon minced ginger
- 1 tablespoon dry sherry or rice wine
- ½ teaspoon sugar
- Pinch white pepper
- 2 teaspoons cornstarch paste

VEGETABLES
- 10 pieces Chinese broccoli stems, trimmed and diagonally cut into 2-inch-long pieces
- 1 celery stalk, halved length wise, trimmed of strings, cut into ¾ x 1-inch pieces (see Notes)
- 12 fancy-cut carrot pieces (page 216-217)
- 12 canned or fresh straw mushrooms
- 12 cloud ears, reconstituted, tough parts trimmed off
- 12 canned gingko nuts
- 2 lily bulbs, trimmed, layers separated (see Notes)
- 2 cups chicken broth, for blanching
- 3 cups vegetable oil, for oil-blanching
- 8 fancy-cut pieces ginger (page 216-217)
- 1 tablespoon oil

Combine prawns with MARINADE ingredients in a bowl in the order listed, mixing well after each addition. Set aside.

Combine SAUCE ingredients in a bowl.

Prepare VEGETABLES and place in separate piles on another plate.

To water-blanch, heat 2 cups chicken broth to a boil in a wok. Add Chinese broccoli and blanch for 1 minute to slightly soften stems. Add celery, carrots and remaining VEGETABLES and blanch for 30 seconds. They should remain crisp-tender. Remove to a colander to drain. (Broth may be saved for another use. Store in refrigerator.)

To oil-blanch, heat 3 cups of oil to 300° in a wok. Add prawns, stirring gently to separate. Blanch prawns for 1½ minutes until they turn slightly opaque and pink. Remove and drain. Set aside.

To stir-fry, remove all but 3 tablespoons of oil from wok. Reheat oil over medium heat. Add ginger and stir for a few seconds until fragrant. Add VEGETABLES and stir for 30 seconds. Add prawns and SAUCE. Toss to coat everything with SAUCE. Stir in 1 tablespoon oil to provide sheen. Transfer to your best platter to serve.

• *Notes* •

1. Fresh lily bulbs are found pre-packaged in plastic bags. They are about 1 inch in diameter and look like small boiling onions. Trim off brown or dry parts at the top and bottom and separate the layers before using. They have a delicate, starchy, raw potato-like texture with a soft crunch.

2. Celery stalks can be made tender by removing the stringy side of the stalk with a potato peeler or knife before cutting into pieces. This makes celery very presentable to an empress!

3. If Chinese broccoli is not available, sugar snap or snow peas are excellent substitutes.

Chef Chu's Lovers' Prawns

Here's a doubly delicious recipe serving red hot, spicy dry-braised prawns with delicate, crystal light prawns in white wine sauce. Both are presented on the same plate, suggesting that a pair of lovers might have different tastes.

Makes: 8 servings
Cooking time: 15 minutes

1 pound medium-size prawns (26 to 30 count)

MARINADE
¼ teaspoon salt
Pinch white pepper
1 egg white
3 teaspoons cornstarch
1 tablespoon vegetable oil

1 green onion

Vegetable oil, for blanching

SAUCE #1
¼ cup chicken broth
1 tablespoon dry sherry
¼ teaspoon salt
¼ teaspoon sugar
½ teaspoon cornstarch paste

SAUCE #2
2 tablespoons catsup
1 tablespoon dry sherry
1 teaspoon sugar
Pinch salt
1 teaspoon soy sauce

1 tablespoon cooked peas
2 tablespoons minced white onion

½ teaspoon minced fresh ginger
1 clove garlic, minced or pressed
1 teaspoon chili paste

Cornstarch paste

¼ teaspoon sesame oil
Sliced tomato
Chinese parsley (cilantro)

Shell, devein, and rinse prawns. Pat dry and split in half. Combine MARINADE ingredients with prawns in the order listed. Let stand for 10 minutes.

Cut lower white part of green onions into ½-inch pieces; coarsely chop upper green part. Set aside.

To oil-blanch, set wok over high heat for about 1 minute. Add 4 cups oil and heat to 300°. Add prawns, stir to separate, and blanch until pink; remove and drain. Combine ingredients for SAUCE #1, then SAUCE #2 in separate bowls.

To stir-fry, remove all but 1 tablespoon oil from wok. Heat oil and add peas, lower part of green onion, half the prawns, and sauce #1. Mix well until hot and thickened; transfer to one side of serving platter.

Quickly, wipe wok clean and heat 2 table-spoons oil. Add white onion, ginger, garlic, and chili paste; stir-fry for 15 seconds. Add remaining prawns, upper part of green onion, and sauce #2. Bring to a boil, mix well, and thicken with about 1 teaspoon cornstarch paste. Sprinkle with sesame oil and transfer to other half of plat-ter. Use tomato slices as divider between prawns and garnish with parsley.

• Note •

Timing is crucial! Have everything ready—including your serving platter with tomato slices—so that the dish can be served hot.

Candied Pecans With Prawns   *Pictured on facing page*

When you taste this dish, you'll find it hard to decide which ingredient you like best: the prawns or the candied pecans. Together, they are close to being magic as the all-time favorite dish on our menu.

Makes: 8 to 10 servings
Cooking time: 5 to 7 minutes

1   pound jumbo prawns
    (16 to 20 count),
    shelled, deveined,
    rinsed and patted dry

MARINADE

¼   teaspoon salt
2   pinches white pepper
1   egg white
2   tablespoons cornstarch
1   tablespoon flour
1   tablespoon vegetable oil

LIGHT MUSTARD SAUCE

½   cup mayonnaise
1½ teaspoons hot Chinese
    Mustard Sauce
    (page 212)
2   tablespoons canned
    sweetened condensed
    milk, honey or sugar
1½ tablespoons fresh
    lemon juice

¼   small head cabbage,
    finely shredded
1   English cucumber
1   unpeeled apple, cored
    and cut into ¾-inch
    chunks (optional)

1   quart vegetable oil, for
    deep-frying

1   cup Hunan Candied
    Pecans (page 43),
    prepared in advance

Place prawns in a medium bowl. Add MARINADE ingredients in the order listed, mixing well after each addition. Set aside. Mix LIGHT MUSTARD SAUCE ingredients in a small bowl; set aside.

To garnish, line the center of a round serving platter with cabbage. Slice cucumber in half lengthwise. Thinly slice cucumbers crosswise and line outside edge of platter with overlapping slices; set aside. Add apple and toss with a little lemon juice to prevent browning. Cover and set aside.

To deep-fry, heat 1 quart oil in a wok to 350°. Place half of the prawns gently in a wok. Cook for about 45 to 60 seconds until prawns turn pink. Remove and drain well. Repeat with remaining prawns.

To deep-fry again, reheat oil to 375°. Return all prawns to oil and fry 1 minute to produce a light crust. Remove prawns and drain well. Place prawns and apple in a large mixing bowl. Toss with enough LIGHT MUSTARD SAUCE to coat lightly. (For suggestions on how to use extra SAUCE, see Notes.)

To serve, arrange prawns over cabbage. Place Candied Pecans around the outside edge of the prawns just before serving.

• *Notes* •

1. The double-frying process produces a light crisp texture on the outside of the prawns and ensures that they are cooked inside and sealed.

2. Candied Pecans should not be placed directly over the prawns because the moisture will soften the candied coating.

3. Leftover LIGHT MUSTARD SAUCE may be stored in an airtight container in the refrigerator and used for other salads or as a dipping sauce for steamed crab, prawns or lobster. Add a little curry powder to change the flavor.

Shanghai Braised Whole Fish

The artful combination of pork, black mushrooms, ginger, garlic, onion, bamboo shoots, spices, and a fresh plump fish made this dish very popular in cosmopolitan Shanghai.

Makes: 6 to 8 servings
Cooking time: 20 minutes

 5 dried black mushrooms

 1 rock cod or red snapper
    (2 to 3 lbs.), cleaned

 6 tablespoons vegetable oil
 1 thumb-size slice fresh
    ginger

 2 tablespoons vegetable oil
 1 ounce pork butt, thinly
    sliced

SPICES

 ¼ small white onion, thinly
    sliced
10 thumb-size slices fresh
    ginger
 4 cloves garlic, minced or
    pressed

 ⅓ cup sliced bamboo shoots

SEASONINGS

 ¼ cup soy sauce
 3 tablespoons dry sherry
 1 tablespoon sugar
    Pinch white pepper
 3 cups water

 2 green onions, cut into
    1½-inch pieces
    Cornstarch paste

Soak mushrooms in warm water for 20 minutes; drain, remove stems, and cut in half. Make several slashes on both sides of fish about ½-inch deep. Rinse and pat dry.

To pan-fry, heat wok (or wide frying pan) over high heat for 1 minute. Add 6 tablespoons oil and swirl to coat sides. Rub wok with slice of ginger. Add fish and fry for 3 to 4 minutes, turning fish once and tipping wok occasionally so that oil touches entire fish. Remove and drain; discard oil and ginger.

To braise, heat clean wok over high heat for about 1 minute. Add 2 tablespoons oil and swirl to coat sides. When oil is hot, add pork, stirring to separate. Add SPICES and cook until fragrant. Stir in bamboo, mushrooms, and SEASONING ingredients. Return fish, cover, reduce heat, and simmer for 7 to 8 minutes. Turn fish over, cover, and simmer for 5 minutes longer. Remove fish to serving platter.

To the sauce, add green onion; thicken with 1½ tablespoons cornstarch paste.

To serve, pour sauce over fish and offer immediately.

• Notes •

1. I prefer snapper or cod because the bones are larger and therefore easier to remove.

2. I never mind repeating my instructions for selecting fresh fish: look for clear eyes, pink gills, a firm touch, and a fresh smell.

3. Lightly pan-frying a whole fish makes it more manageable or slightly firmer; that's important so it won't fall apart during the braising process.

4. Sometimes I add bean cake—it absorbs the flavor of the fish beautifully.

Miso-crusted Sea Bass   *Pictured on page 215*

This dish is easy to make but has a huge impact on guests! The sea bass is juicy and succulent inside and lightly encrusted with glaze on top; the slightly sweet-salty glaze beautifully balances the richness of the fish.

Makes: 4 servings
Cooking time: 14 to 16 minutes, depending on thickness of fish

1½ pounds whole single-piece Chilean Sea Bass fillet (allow one 6-ounce fillet per person for individual serving)

MARINADE
½ cup white miso
½ cup red miso
6 tablespoons honey
2 tablespoons minced fresh ginger
¼ cup mirin

Banana leaf or ti leaves
Chinese parsley (cilantro) sprigs or tropical flower (optional)

Rinse sea bass and pat dry. Set aside. Combine MARINADE ingredients in a bowl with a whisk and mix well. Place sea bass in a bowl. Brush MARINADE to coat all sides of the sea bass. Place sea bass in a sealed plastic bag. Marinate sea bass in the sealed bag in the refrigerator for at least 30 minutes, or several hours to overnight.

To broil, preheat broiler to 500°. Coat a cooking rack with oil or non-stick spray on a foil-lined cooking sheet. Place sea bass on the rack. Set oven rack in the middle of the oven about 6 to 8 inches from broiler. Broil fish for 5 minutes, until browned along the edges. Turn over and brush with MARINADE. Broil another 5 minutes until done and golden brown. The sea bass should still be moist and juicy inside. Do not overcook (see Notes). Test for doneness with a fork or chopstick inserted in the thickest part of the fillet; it should go through easily. The MARINADE should caramelize and form a shiny glazed crust on the surface of the fish.

To serve, line a platter with a banana leaf or ti leaves. Place fillet in the center and garnish with Chinese parsley sprigs or a tropical flower. The sea bass should be tender enough for diners to cut off a portion for themselves with a serving spoon. For individual entrees, place a 6-ounce fillet on each individual plate and garnish with Chinese parsley.

• *Notes* •

1. Use enough marinade to coat the fish. Save unused marinade for another time. The marinade keeps well, stored in an airtight container in the refrigerator, for up to 3 weeks.

2. Broiling time and doneness depends on thickness of fillet and its temperature before broiling, so times given here are approximate

Hangchow Poached Fish

Delicately poached fresh rock cod topped with slivers of green onion and ginger whose flavors are quickly released just before serving is a memorable dish reminiscent of great restaurants on the shores of West Lake in the resort town of Hangchow.

Makes: 6 to 8 servings
Cooking time: 25 minutes

- 1 whole fish, such as rock cod or red snapper (2 to 3 lbs.), cleaned
- 2 green onions, cut into fourths
- 4 thumb-size slices fresh ginger

SEASONINGS

- ¼ cup soy sauce
- 3 green onions (white part), slivered
- 3 thumb-size slices fresh ginger, slivered
  Pinch white pepper

- ½ cup vegetable oil
- 1 tablespoon sesame oil
  Chinese parsley (cilantro)

Remove fins from fish, if necessary. From head to tail, cut a slash on both sides of fish about 1 inch below the backbone.

To poach, heat wok over moderate heat and when hot, add onion and ginger. Stir-fry until fragrant. Pour about 2 quarts water into wok, bring to a boil, then immerse fish (add more boiling water, if necessary). Return to a boil, reduce heat, cover, and simmer for 10 minutes. Turn fish over and boil for about 5 minutes longer. Remove carefully with a spatula and drain well. Place fish on serving platter.

To serve, sprinkle SEASONINGS all over fish. Heat oils in a small saucepan until hot and just smoking. Quickly pour over fish and garnish with parsley. Lightly mix pieces of fish with sauce at the table and serve.

• *Notes* •

1. Only the best ingredients—good quality fresh fish and seasonings—should be used in any simple poaching recipe such as this.

2. Poaching time for fish needs to be accurate. I check for doneness this way: the meat is still slightly rare near the bone yet flaky and easy to remove on the outside.

Steamed Kirin Fish

Kirin was a mythical creature said to be half dragon and half lion. Our presentation of Steamed Kirin Fish is a colorful one: thin slices of ham, black mushroom, and ginger are tucked into pockets cut along the sides of a whole fish.

Makes: 8 to 10 servings
Cooking time: 30 minutes

  5 or 6 dried black
    mushrooms

  1 rock cod or red snapper
    (about 3 lbs.), or 1 piece
    of Ling cod

 10 to 12 pieces Virginia ham
    (sliced ⅛-inch by 1-inch)
 10 to 12 slices fresh ginger
  1 tablespoon dry sherry
 1½ teaspoons salt
  1 green onion, crushed
    slightly
  1 piece caul fat

Soak mushrooms in warm water for 20 minutes; drain, remove stems, and cut in half.

Remove head of fish (if desired) and trim off tail. Starting at the head, make 10 to 12 slashes about 1-inch apart the length of the fish. Only do this on one side and make sure you don't cut through the backbone. Rinse and pat dry.

To assemble, tuck 1 slice ham, 1 slice ginger, and 1 piece mushroom into each slash. Sprinkle entire fish with sherry and salt. Place on a footed plate suitable for steaming. Lay green onion on fish and drape caul fat over top, tucking excess under the edges.

To steam, place plate in steamer; cover and steam over boiling water for 20 minutes. Remove and place plate on top of serving platter for easier handling. Discard onion and caul fat before serving. Offer juices to spoon over.

• *Notes* •

1. Caul fat is optional but I strongly recommend it. (See page 201, for more information.) You may have to order it in advance from your butcher.

2. I like to specify Rock or Ling cod or red snapper for this dish because they have fewer bones than other varieties.

3. For a different presentation, cut the fish in the pattern pictured on page 103.

Dragon Fish *Pictured on facing page*

Dragon Fish, symbolizing prosperity and happiness, is a speciality dish usually reserved for banquets or other festive occasions. It is garnished with red cherries suggesting good luck to Chinese people, and is an item that I gladly prepare.

Makes: 6 to 8 servings
Cooking time: 20 minutes

1 whole red snapper or rock cod (4 to 5 lbs.), cleaned
Dash salt

BATTER
1 cup flour
1 cup cornstarch
1½ cups water
1 tablespoon vegetable oil

Vegetable oil, for deep-frying

1½ cups Sweet & Sour Sauce (page 213)
Cornstarch paste

2 olives
1 lemon, sliced
2 cherries
1 can (10 oz.) preserved cucumber slices, drained OR a combination of 2 tablespoons green peas, 2 diced black mushrooms, ¼ diced white onion, ½ chopped tomato, and some diced carrot.

Remove fish head and reserve. Prepare fish according to illustrations on facing page. After cutting, hold fish by tail and immerse in lukewarm water until pattern shows up. Pat dry and sprinkle with salt.

Combine BATTER ingredients in a bowl until the consistency of heavy cream is reached.

To deep-fry, heat 4 cups oil in a wok to 350°. Coat fish head in batter and deep-fry in oil until golden brown. Remove, drain, and place on serving plate. Return oil temperature to 350°. Turn fish inside out and hold by its tail to dip into batter. Make sure all the scored (patterned) flesh is covered with batter. Let excess drip off.

With fish still inside out, grasp both ends and slowly immerse fish in oil. Deep-fry, basting occasionally and turning so that oil reaches all sides, for about 8 minutes or until golden brown. With a spatula or strainer, carefully remove and set aside. (The above procedure may be done in advance.)

Prepare Sweet & Sour Sauce, thicken with about 3 tablespoons cornstarch paste.

To deep-fry again, reheat oil in wok to 350°. Add fish and fry for about 3 minutes, basting occasionally. Carefully, remove with spatula or strainer and place on serving platter. Arrange fish head to recreate original shape.

To serve, place olives in the eyes and place lemon slices topped with cherries around edge of plate. Ladle sauce over fish; sprinkle with preserved cucumber. Serve immediately.

• *Notes* •

1. The fish is immersed in water before coated with batter to slightly shrink the flesh and cause the scored diamond pattern to show up.

2. Make sure that the fish is completely pat dry before deep-frying; just a little bit of water can cause splattering.

3. A spatula or strainer used for removing the fish from the oil is important since the fish will be flaky and could fall apart.

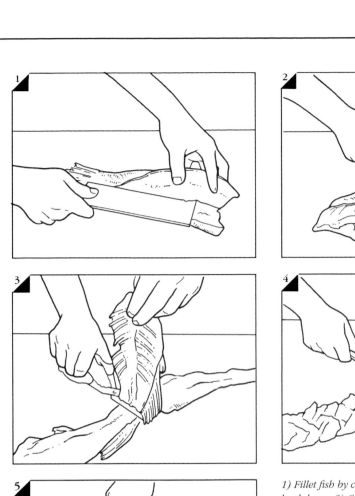

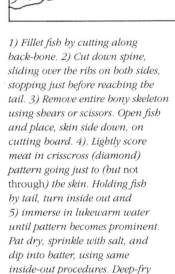

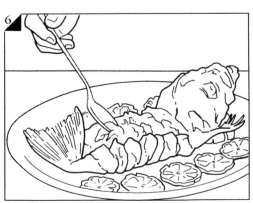

1) Fillet fish by cutting along back-bone. 2) Cut down spine, sliding over the ribs on both sides, stopping just before reaching the tail. 3) Remove entire bony skeleton using shears or scissors. Open fish and place, skin side down, on cutting board. 4). Lightly score meat in crisscross (diamond) pattern going just to (but not through) the skin. Holding fish by tail, turn inside out and 5) immerse in lukewarm water until pattern becomes prominent. Pat dry, sprinkle with salt, and dip into batter, using same inside-out procedures. Deep-fry as directed and 6) arrange on platter, with patterned, meaty side out. Decorate and ladle sauce over fish to serve.

Grilled Scallops With Garlic Sauce

These scallops can be grilled on a very hot charcoal grill, pan-seared on a ridged skillet or stove top grill—any method will produce excellent grill marks on the scallops. Water chestnuts, green onions and chili paste give the spicy, garlicky sauce an interesting texture.

Makes: 8 to 10 servings
Cooking time: 10 to 12 minutes

1½   pounds (10 to 20 count) large
     Eastern sea scallops

MARINADE

     Pinch salt and white pepper
1   egg white
2   tablespoons cornstarch

SEASONING SAUCE

½   cup chicken broth
3   tablespoons soy sauce
1   tablespoon white distilled
     vinegar
1   tablespoon Shao Hsing wine
1   tablespoon sugar

     Vegetable oil for grill

2   tablespoons vegetable oil

SPICES

5   slices ginger, minced
5   or 6 cloves garlic, minced
     (to taste)
4   water chestnuts, coarsely
     chopped
1   to 2 tablespoons chili paste
     (to taste)

1   tablespoon cornstarch paste

1   tablespoon sesame oil

3   green onions (white part),
     minced

Briefly rinse scallops under cold water. Drain and pat dry. Transfer scallops to a bowl and add MARINADE ingredients in the order listed. Mix well and set aside for 30 minutes. Combine SEASONING SAUCE in a small bowl.

To grill, place scallops on a very hot, oiled grill and cook about 1½ to 2 minutes on each side until seared with brown grill marks. Do not overcook. Remove and drain.

To stir-fry, heat a wok until hot and add 2 tablespoons oil. Add ginger and garlic; stir a few seconds until fragrant. Add water chestnuts and stir for 30 seconds to heat through. Add chili paste and SEASONING SAUCE and bring to a boil. Thicken with cornstarch paste to a medium light consistency. Stir in sesame oil and green onions.

To serve, pour sauce onto a rimmed serving platter. Place scallops with the best grill marks facing upward in a single layer on top of sauce.

• Notes •

1. When purchasing scallops, allow 2 pieces per person. Use large sea scallops which are at least 1½-inches in diameter and at least ¾ to 1-inch thick. You can substitute large or giant peeled prawns, or firm fish filets cut into 2-inch squares, for the scallops in this dish. Marinate as directed for the scallops.

2. Pan-sear the scallops in a heavy skillet or wok with a small amount of oil, if you do not have a grill. To serve, lightly spoon sauce over scallops and serve.

Foochow Steamed Clams

Here is a seacoast delicacy: freshly caught clams smothered in black beans, garlic, ginger, green onion, and sherry. Aromatic and delicious.

Makes: 6 to 8 servings
Cooking time: 10 minutes

2 pounds fresh clams (24 to 26 count)
½ teaspoon oil

3 tablespoons vegetable oil

SEASONINGS
1 tablespoon dry sherry
1 tablespoon soy sauce
½ cup chicken broth
1 teaspoon sugar
Pinch white pepper

SPICES
1 tablespoon fermented black beans, smashed
2 cloves garlic, sliced
4 thumb-size slices fresh ginger, shredded
½ teaspoon chili paste (optional)

1 green onion, chopped
Cornstarch paste
¼ teaspoon sesame oil

In a large bowl, cover clams with cold water mixed with ½ teaspoon oil. Soak for 2 hours in order for clams to spew out the sand.

To water-blanch, drop clams in boiling water and blanch for 2 minutes. Remove and drain, discarding those clams that did not open.

Combine SEASONINGS and set aside.

To stir-fry, heat wok (or wide frying pan) over high heat for 1 minute until hot. Add oil and swirl pan to coat sides. When oil is hot, add SPICES and stir-fry for about 30 seconds until fragrant. Return clams to wok, add SEASONINGS, stir gently and cover for about 1 minute or until all clam shells are more widely opened. Add onion and stir for 1 minute. Without causing meat to pop out of clams, thicken slightly with 1 to 2 teaspoons cornstarch paste until the consistency of cream soup is reached. Sprinkle with sesame oil.

To serve, place clams and sauce in a wide serving bowl deep enough to hold all the sauce.

• *Notes* •

1. Eliminate the chili paste if you prefer a dish with less spice.

2. When buying fresh clams, choose only the freshest ones that are closed shut. Ones that have opened—even slightly—are dead!

Canton Ginger Sherry Crab

Though not actually baked, this crab is so succulent and flavorful you'll think it's been cooked in the oven.

Makes: 4 servings
Cooking time: 20 minutes

- 1 fresh crab (1½ to 2 lbs.), cleaned and cracked
- 2 thumb-size pieces fresh ginger
- 1 tablespoon dry sherry
- 3 tablespoons flour

  Vegetable oil, for deep-frying

SAUCE

- 1 cup Rich Chicken Broth (page 52), or chicken bouillon
- 2 tablespoons dry sherry
- 2 tablespoons soy sauce
- 1 teaspoon sugar
- 5 thumb-size pieces fresh ginger
- 1 green onion, cut into 1-inch pieces

  Cornstarch paste

Combine crab, ginger, and sherry together; let stand for 10 minutes. Remove crab, discarding any ginger clinging to sides. Dust lightly with flour.

To deep-fry, heat 3 cups oil in a wok (or electric deep-fat fryer) to 350°. Add crab and fry, stirring occasionally, for about 5 minutes or until browned. Remove and drain.

Combine SAUCE ingredients in a small bowl; set aside.

To stir-fry, remove all but 4 tablespoons oil from wok. Heat, swirling wok to coat sides. Add ginger and green onion; cook until fragrant. Return crab to wok. Pour in sauce, cover, and cook over high heat for about 5 to 7 minutes or until sauce is reduced by one-fourth. Thicken with 1 tablespoon cornstarch paste to serve.

• *Note* •

This dish calls for fresh *live* crab. If you don't like to remove the shell of a live crab, ask your fish market to do so. Or, drop it into boiling water for 30 seconds and then clean.

Dungeness Crab With Golden Garlic Crust

My poetic name for this dish is "crab hiding in sand." The panko topping is redolent of garlic and a touch of spicy jalapeño.   *Pictured on page 88, 214*

Makes: 4 servings
Cooking time: 15 to 20 minutes

1   (2 to 2½ pound) fresh
    live crab, scrubbed
½   cup cornstarch, for
    dredging

GARLIC CRUMBS

1   cup panko bread
    crumbs
1   teaspoon dried red chili
    flakes
½   cup vegetable oil
¼   cup minced garlic cloves
½   teaspoon salt
1   quart vegetable oil

SPICES

1   red jalapeño chile,
    coarsely chopped
    (with seeds if you like
    it hotter)
1   green onion, chopped
2   tablespoons rice wine
1   tablespoon sesame oil
5   sprigs Chinese parsley
    (cilantro)

To serve, arrange legs and claws on a large platter to resemble crab shape; place head shell on top. Sprinkle panko crumbs over crab. Garnish with Chinese parsley.

To prepare the crab, remove and discard bottom flap. Scrub flap area, bottom and top side of the head shell. Put your thumbs between the rear shell and head section and pull them apart. Discard spongy matter, intestines and mouth flaps. Rinse inside of shell. Leave in the ivory crab butter. Rinse shell again.

Twist off the claws and separate each into claws and knuckles. Cut central body lengthwise making two halves, each with legs attached. Cut between each leg, so each leg will have a portion of the central body attached. Crack claws and legs lightly with the side of a cleaver so shells remain intact. Dredge exposed crab meat (not shells) with cornstarch; dust the inside of head shell. Place SPICES on a small plate.

To toast panko, heat a dry wok or frying pan over medium-low heat. Add panko and dried chili flakes. Stir constantly until crumbs turn evenly golden tan. Watch carefully. When you smell the aroma of toasted chili and the panko turns evenly, golden tan, transfer to a bowl. Set aside.

To shallow-fry garlic, heat ½ cup oil in a wok to 300°. Add garlic. Stir about 1 to 1½ minutes until garlic loses its sizzle (moisture), turns golden (not brown) and no longer clings together. Pour garlic through a fine strainer set over a bowl. Immediately add garlic and salt to panko. Toss until crumbs turn, dry, crisp and very aromatic. Set aside. (Can be kept airtight for 1 or 2 days.)

To deep-fry, heat 1 quart oil in a wok to 365°. Working in 3 or 4 batches, place crab in hot oil and deep-fry 1 to 1½ minutes until a golden light crust forms. Slightly undercook the crab. Remove and drain. Reheat oil for 30 seconds between batches. Fry remaining crab. Fry top shell last open side up, spooning a little oil inside. Drain with open side down. (Can be done up to 30 minutes ahead.)

To deep-fry again, clean the wok and oil of all residue. Reheat the oil to 375°. Deep-fry crab (head shell does not have to be refried) in two batches for 30 to 45 seconds each. Drain.

To stir-fry, remove all but 3 tablespoons of oil from wok. Reheat oil over high heat until lightly smoking. Add SPICES and stir-fry for 30 seconds. Add crab, wine and sesame oil and toss for 30 seconds. Add GARLIC CRUMBS and toss for 30 seconds until crab is lightly coated.

Maine Lobster Yee-mein   *Pictured on facing page*

Maine lobster is sought after for its sweet-tasting meat. We prepare it with a delicious sauce and *yee-mein* noodles to soak up the flavorful goodness. Our eye-catching presentation makes it a first-class entrée.

Makes: 4 servings
Cooking time: 30 minutes

2 (1½ pound) live Maine lobsters, lightly scrubbed

BROTH

2 quarts chicken broth
3 green onions, crushed
1 knob ginger, crushed
½ teaspoon salt
1 tablespoon rice wine or dry sherry
1 round dried *yee-mein* noodles (page 207)
1 cup vegetable oil, for shallow-frying
2 tablespoons cornstarch, for dredging

SPICES

2 green onions (white part), minced
4 ginger slices, minced

SEASONING SAUCE

2 cups reserved broth
1 tablespoon oyster sauce
1 tablespoon rice wine or dry sherry
½ teaspoon sugar
¼ teaspoon salt
¼ teaspoon white pepper (to taste)
2 tablespoons cornstarch paste
1 tablespoon oil
Chinese parsley (cilantro) sprigs for garnish

• *Note* •

Julienned zucchini, yellow squash, colorful bell peppers or carrot can be braised for 1½ minutes at the end of braising the noodles to add color, texture, and nutrients to the dish.

To prepare lobster, pull apart lobsters between the tail and head section. Separate underbelly and legs from head. Cut claw pieces into two sections, separating knuckles from claws. Discard the insides of the head and rinse thoroughly. Cut head shell in half lengthwise. Cut off legs from underbody. Discard underbelly. Lightly crack legs. Place claws, knuckles, legs and head sections in a bowl to make BROTH.

Using a cleaver, split tail sections lengthwise in half. Set tails aside on a separate plate.

To cook, bring BROTH ingredients to a boil in a wok. Simmer for 3 minutes Add claws, knuckles, legs and head sections. Cover lobster pieces with broth to maximize flavor. Return BROTH to a boil; simmer for 10 minutes. Remove lobster pieces to a plate with a wire strainer. Strain BROTH through a fine mesh sieve, discarding shells and solids. Reserve BROTH.

Use kitchen shears to remove meat intact from the knuckles and claws. Set meat aside. Rinse head shells; set aside for garnish. Discard all other cooked shells.

To braise, bring reserved BROTH to a boil in a wok. Add noodles. Return BROTH to a boil. Braise for 1 minute. Lift out noodles; drain well. Reserve BROTH. Keep noodles warm in a bowl.

Combine 2 cups reserved broth with remaining SEASONING SAUCE ingredients in a bowl. Set aside.

To shallow-fry, heat 1 cup vegetable oil to 365° in a wok. Lightly dredge the meaty surfaces of lobster tails with 2 tablespoons cornstarch. Place, meaty side down, in oil. Pan-fry 1 minute until a golden crust is formed. Turn once and pan-fry other side for 1 minute. Remove and drain.

To stir-fry, remove all but 2 tablespoons of oil from wok. Reheat oil, add SPICES and stir for a few seconds until fragrant. Add SEASONING SAUCE and bring to a boil. Add knuckles, claw meat and tails. Stir for 1½ to 2 minutes. Adjust seasonings. Thicken with enough cornstarch paste to make a light sauce. Stir in 1 tablespoon oil. Remove from heat.

To serve, divide noodles onto individual serving plates. Place a lobster tail, meaty side up, in the center of noodles. Tuck knuckles and a claw on either side of the tail. Spoon SAUCE over lobster and noodles. Garnish each serving with a half head shell placed vertically so head and feelers are pointing upward and a sprig of Chinese parsley.

PORK

Without question, pork is the meat most favored by Chinese. It is flavorful and very versatile, since it can be cooked in a great many ways and even assumes a background disguise when cooked with other ingredients, such as fish, crab, or lobster.

The recipes in this section include the great American favorite, Sweet & Sour Pork. I have added my "secret" to this dish, so follow the instructions carefully. I have also included the recipe ranked number one by patrons of my restaurant: Mu Shu Pork. If you are vegetarian, the notes following the recipe tell you how to make variations without using meat.

When buying pork, choose meat that is deep pink with very white fat and skin. The marble grain should be firm and bounce back when touched. If the fat is wet and the meat has a dull or dark color, it has been frozen too long; if the meat has a strong odor and feels sticky, it is beginning to spoil.

For overall versatility, I recommend buying *pork shoulder butt*. It can be cut into slices, shredded or cubed, as for Sweet & Sour Pork, julienned into long strips for Mu Shu Pork, sliced for Barbecued Pork, or purchased in a 3- to 4-pound block and ground up as filling in Won-ton, Cucumber Cups, Shanghai Braised Fish, Lion's Head in a Clay Pot, and many other dishes. Ask your butcher to grind the pork for you, then bag it in 2-inch-square blocks and freeze it until needed. (This is far preferable to buying pork that has already been ground.) The ratio of fat to lean in ground pork is up to you, so instruct your butcher accordingly.

Spareribs generally come in large racks ranging from 4 to 5 pounds. You may ask your butcher to cut them into individual ribs or strips.

Whole roast pig is a favorite delicacy that requires a special oven. Chinese food enthusiasts can recommend a delicatessen where roast meats and poultry are sold. Drop in and you will see whole freshly roasted pigs displayed along with hanging ducks and roast pork. Purchase a piece of the pig and be sure it has some crackling crisp skin on top. It is best to eat roast pig while it is still warm, with a drizzle of oyster sauce or a dip of plum sauce. That's heaven!

Orange Blossom Ribs (page 128) are slow-braised in a piquant sauce that makes the meat fork-soft and succulent.

Mongolian Firepot   *Pictured on facing page*

Excellent to serve at your next dinner party, this meal is cooked right at the table and by your guests! The fiery brass kettle adds a touch of drama to the presentation, and the array of thinly-sliced meat and fish, shrimp, and many vegetables fill the table and promise a delectable feast.

Makes: 8 to 12 servings
Cooking time: 30 minutes

4 quarts Rich Chicken Broth (page 52), or chicken bouillon

INGREDIENTS
(Allow 2 to 4 ounces of each per person)

Slices of fish filet such as snapper or rock cod
Slices of leg of lamb
Slices of shelled, deveined, and butterflied prawns
Slices of sirloin beef and lean pork
Bite-size pieces of fresh spinach
Bite-size pieces of bean cake (tofu)
Presoaked pieces of bean thread
Bite-size wedges of Chinese cabbage

SAUCES
Soy sauce
Chinese barbecue sauce
Hot Chili Paste (page 212)
Rice vinegar

Arrange fish and meat attractively on individual serving plates. Arrange vegetables together on one large serving platter.

To assemble, start charcoal in firepot braiser outdoors. When red hot, bring braiser indoors and place on wet towel on top of heat-resistant platter. Heat chicken broth on stove and when hot, pour about 2 quarts into firepot.

To cook, provide individual strainers for each guest to use. Blanch food by immersing into boiling broth until desired doneness is reached. Offer SAUCES for dipping at the table as well. Towards end of meal, offer broth in individual bowls for sipping.

• *Notes* •

1. The nice feature about cooking with a firepot is that the quantity of ingredients can be changed depending on how many people you're serving.

2. I enjoy offering other ingredients suchas fresh squid, oysters, shrimp balls, bite-size wedges of romaine lettuce, or any other type of food available.

Brass Mongolian firepot transforms into bubbling centerpiece for this cook-your-own Chinese dinner. Guests select from platters displaying paper-thin slices of meat and fish, vegetables, and bite-size pieces of bean curd and bean thread. When all is cooked, guests ladle out flavorful cooking broth into soup bowls.

Sweet & Sour Pork

Sweet, sour, pungent, and crunchy—an unbeatable combination. The secret to preparing this correctly is in the double-frying.

Makes: 6 to 8 servings
Cooking time: 20 minutes

1½ cups Sweet & Sour Sauce (page 213)

1 pound pork shoulder butt, boned, trimmed, and cut into ¾-inch cubes

MARINADE

1 teaspoon dry sherry
1 teaspoon garlic powder
½ teaspoon salt
Pinch Chinese five-spice

BATTER

½ cup flour
½ cup cornstarch
¼ teaspoon baking powder
1 cup water
1 teaspoon oil

Vegetable oil, for deep-frying

3 tablespoons vegetable oil

VEGETABLES

1 bell pepper, seeded and cut into bite-size squares
¼ small white onion, cut in bite-size squares
5 to 6 thin slices carrot
½ cup pineapple chunks
Cornstarch paste

Prepare Sweet & Sour Sauce as directed.

Combine pork and MARINADE ingredients; let stand for 30 minutes. Mix together BATTER ingredients until the consistency of heavy cream; let stand for 15 minutes. Just before using, stir to mix; pour enough batter over pork to coat.

To deep-fry, heat 4 cups oil in a wok (or electric deep-fat fryer) to 325°. Add half the pork and cook for about 3 minutes or until a crust is formed. Repeat with remaining pork. Remove and drain. (You can do the above procedure ahead of time, if desired.)

To deep-fry again, remove any pieces of batter left in oil and raise temperature in wok to 350° to 375°. Return pork and agitate (carefully shake) to separate. Deep-fry until golden brown; remove and drain oil in wok.

To hot mix, heat wok over high heat for 1 minute. Add 3 tablespoons oil and then sauce, VEGETABLES, and pineapple. Bring to a boil and thicken with 2 tablespoons cornstarch paste. Add pork, mix well, and serve.

• *Notes* •

1. For variety, you can add lichee nuts, loquats, cherries, tomatoes, or other fresh fruits or vegetables to this recipe.

2. To retain the crunchy texture of the deep-fried pork, it's important to "hot mix" quickly. You're trying to coat the pork, not cook it.

Mu Shu Pork   *Pictured on page 116*

Mu Shu is the name of a tree found in Northern China that bears beautiful yellow flowers. When the eggs in this dish are quickly cooked in a preheated wok, they puff up and blossom, resembling the Mu Shu flower. Vegetarians can leave out the pork and still have a flavorful dish.

Makes: 6 to 8 servings
Cooking time: 15 minutes

  1 large tree mushroom
  ¼ cup tiger lily buds
  ½ pound pork shoulder butt, cut into ⅛- by ⅛- by 1½-inch strips

MARINADE
  1 teaspoon soy sauce
  ¼ teaspoon cornstarch
  1 tablespoon vegetable oil

 12 Mandarin Pancakes (page 187) or paper-thin pancakes made with flour

  ½ cup vegetable oil
  3 eggs, slightly beaten
  ½ cup shredded bamboo shoots
  ½ head regular cabbage, shredded
  2 green onions, white parts slivered and green tops cut in 1-inch sections

SEASONINGS
  2 tablespoons soy sauce
  ½ teaspoon sugar
  ¼ teaspoon salt
  ¼ teaspoon white pepper
    Dash sesame oil

  4 tablespoons Hoisin sauce
  ½ teaspoon sesame oil

Soak mushroom in warm water for 20 minutes; drain, remove stem, and shred. Soak tiger lily buds in warm water for 20 minutes; drain.

Combine pork with MARINADE ingredients in the order listed; mix well and set aside.

To steam, separate pancakes and fold them in half. Arrange inside a cloth napkin. Place napkin on rack in steamer (or in double boiler) and steam for 3 or 4 minutes. Remove from heat and keep warm and moist in steamer.

To stir-fry, heat wok (or wide frying pan) over high heat for 1 minute until hot. Add oil, swirling to coat sides. When oil is smoking hot, pour in eggs and scramble until golden; remove and drain. Add pork, stir vigorously to separate, and cook until well done. Remove and drain.

Remove all but 3 tablespoons oil. Return pork to wok and add mushrooms, lily buds, and bamboo shoots. Stir-fry for 2 minutes. Add cabbage, green onion, eggs, and SEASONINGS. Mix well and add dash sesame oil. Transfer to platter.

To serve, place green onion slivers on a small plate. Combine Hoisin sauce and sesame oil; place on another small plate. Open wrapper, spread center lightly with sauce mixture and a few slivers green onion. Spoon about 2 tablespoons pork into center of wrapper and fold up, jelly-roll fashion, to eat.

• *Notes* •

1. Time and time again I've found that my guests don't know how to assemble Mu Shu Pork correctly. Since this is a do-it-yourself dish, show them how to make the first one.

2. It's often difficult to keep the pancakes warm so I recommend using a candle (coffee warmer) holder similar to the bottom of a fondue pot. Place a flat pan on top. When your turn comes, quickly reheat your pancake by placing it on top of hot pan for 5 seconds.

3. If you wish, shrimp, chicken, or beef can be substituted for pork.

4. Oil must be smoking hot in order to achieve the correct texture for the scrambled eggs.

Mu Shu Pork, the most requested dish at Chef Chu's restaurant, is easily prepared at home. 1, 2) Scramble eggs in a heated wok, then 3) removed and drain off the oil. 4, 5) Stir-fry strips of marinated pork and then 6) remove and drain. 7) Add shredded cabbage, mushrooms, lily buds, bamboo shoots and green onion, 8) stir-frying as you go. 9) Return cooked eggs and pork; toss gently. Offer steamed Mandarin pancakes to serve.

Pork With Imperial Sauce

This East-meets-West sauce is of my own creation. Highly seasoned, it's sure to satisfy all senses, especially when you hear "delicious"!

Makes: 6 to 8 servings
Cooking time: 1 hour

1 pound pork shoulder butt, boned, trimmed, and cut into ¾-inch cubes

MARINADE

- 1 teaspoon dry sherry
- 1 teaspoon garlic powder
- ½ teaspoon salt
  Pinch Chinese five-spice

BATTER

- ½ cup flour
- ½ cup cornstarch
- ¼ teaspoon baking powder
- 1 cup water
- 1 teaspoon vegetable oil

  Vegetable oil, for deep-frying

SAUCE

- 5 tablespoons chicken broth
- 3 tablespoons catsup
- 2 tablespoons sugar
- 1 tablespoon Worcestershire
- 1 tablespoon soy sauce
- 1 tablespoon A-1 sauce
  Pinch Chinese five-spice

- 2 tablespoons vegetable oil
  Cornstarch paste
- 1 teaspoon sesame oil

  Thin slices tomato
  Chinese Parsley (cilantro)

Combine pork and MARINADE ingredients thoroughly; let stand for 30 minutes.

Mix together BATTER ingredients until the consistency of heavy cream is reached; let stand 15 minutes. Just before using, stir batter to mix. Pour over pork just to coat pieces.

To deep-fry, heat 4 cups oil in a wok (or electric deep-fat fryer) to 325°. Add half the pork and cook for about 3 minutes or until a crust is formed. Repeat with remaining pork. Remove and drain. (You can do the above procedure ahead of time, if desired.)

Combine SAUCE ingredients in a saucepan; bring to a boil, remove, and set aside.

To deep-fry again, remove any pieces of batter left in oil and then raise temperature in wok to 350° to 375°. Return pork and agitate (carefully shake) to separate. Deep-fry until golden brown; remove and drain off oil in wok.

To hot mix, heat wok over high heat for 1 minute. Add 2 tablespoons oil and then sauce. Bring to a boil and thicken with 1½ tablespoons cornstarch paste to a consistency of syrup. Mix in pork until well coated; stir in sesame oil.

To serve, transfer pork to a serving platter and decorate with tomato slices and parsley.

• Note •

To retain the crunchy texture of the deep-fried pork, it's important to "hot mix" quickly. You're trying to coat the pork with sauce, not cook it further.

Chinkiang Pork Chops

Chinkiang is a city known for its unique-tasting dark rice vinegar. The sweet-tart taste of the smothering sauce complements the pork and is delicious with rice.

Makes: 4 servings
Cooking time: 15 minutes

1 pound sliced pork chops (cut ¼-inch thick)
1 quart water
1 teaspoon unseasoned meat tenderizer

MARINADE

1 tablespoon soy sauce
Pinch Five-spice powder
1 egg, beaten
1 tablespoon cornstarch
1 tablespoon flour
1 tablespoon vegetable oil

SAUCE

Juice of 1 orange or ½ cup orange juice
5 tablespoons chicken broth
3 tablespoons catsup
3 tablespoons sugar
3 tablespoons Chinkiang vinegar
1 tablespoon Worcester-shire sauce
1 tablespoon soy sauce
2 teaspoons cornstarch paste

1 orange

3 cups vegetable oil for deep-frying

Cut each pork chop into 2 to 4 pieces, leaving the bones attached (see Notes). Combine water and tenderizer in a large bowl. Add the pork chops and toss well. Cover and refrigerate for 1 hour to tenderize.

Remove pork from refrigerator, drain well, and pat dry. Place pork in bowl and add MARINADE ingredients in the order listed. Mix well and set aside. Combine SAUCE ingredients in another bowl.

To garnish, cut the remaining orange lengthwise in half. Thinly slice orange crosswise, discarding ends. Place overlapping orange slices evenly around the outside rim of a serving platter to form a decorative scalloped edging.

To deep-fry, heat 3 cups of oil to 365° in a wok. Deep-fry pork in 2 or 3 batches. Carefully slide each pork chop down the side of the wok and cook them in a single layer so each piece is as flat as possible. Turn pork chops over and stir gently to prevent pieces from sticking together. Fry for 1 to 2 minutes or until a light golden crust is formed. Remove and drain well. Repeat with remaining pork chops.

To deep-fry again, reheat oil to 365°. Deep-fry pork in 2 batches for 20 to 30 seconds per batch, until medium-brown and a crisp crust is formed. Remove and drain well.

To smother, remove all oil from wok except 1 tablespoon. Add SAUCE; stir constantly until sauce is thickened. Add pork and quickly toss until sauce evenly coats pork chops. Transfer pork to the garnished plate and serve.

• *Notes* •

1. Look for thin ¼-inch sliced pork chops for this dish, or have your butcher cut them for you.

2. Substitute boneless, thinly sliced pork loin for the pork chops if you do not want to deal with bones. If necessary, pound the pork loin lightly to make the meat uniformly thin. You can also substitute thinly sliced lean pork butt, 2-inch long baby back ribs, or crosscut 2-inch long spareribs for the pork chops.

119

Tender slices of carved Virginia ham, sweetened with lotus seeds and fragrant kuei-hua *blossoms, are tucked inside slices of steamed bread in this classic Hunan banquet dish.*

Hunan Honey-glazed Ham   *Pictured on facing page*

Popular in Hunan restaurants, this succulent ham is usually served with bread-like finger sandwiches. The flavors of the lotus seeds, a little sugar, and a dried ingredient called *kuei-hua* combine during the steaming process to create a memorable syrup.

Makes: 6 servings
Cooking time: 45 minutes

- ½ cup lotus seeds
- ¾ pound boneless fresh Smithfield (Virginia) ham
- 12 slices white bread
- 3 tablespoons sugar
- ¼ teaspoon dried *kuei-hua* (osmanthus blossom)

Soak lotus seeds in warm water for 1 hour; then steam over boiling water for about 30 minutes or until soft. Set aside.

If outer skin remains on ham, steam ham over boiling water in steamer for about 30 minutes to soften. Then trim off and discard skin and fat to make pieces of ham measuring 1½ by 2 by 4 inches. Carefully slice pieces ⅛-inch thick.

Slightly freeze bread for easier handling. Trim off crust and cut in half. Split each half almost all the way through lengthwise, forming a pocket. Cover bread with towel to prevent drying and set aside.

To assemble, line the inside of a 6-inch bowl with rows of overlapping slices of ham. Add remaining ham slices and any meat trimmings.

To steam, place ½ cup water in bowl with ham. Put bowl on rack in steamer, cover, and steam over boiling water for 30 minutes. Remove and carefully pour off water. Sprinkle lotus seeds, 2 tablespoons sugar, and *kuei-hua* over ham.

To steam again, place bowl on rack in steamer and steam for 15 to 20 minutes longer. Remove (keeping steamer available for bread), and carefully tip bowl, pouring off juices into a saucepan. Soften bread in steamer for about 1 minute; keep warm.

To serve, quickly bring juices to a boil, add 3 tablespoons water and 2 tablespoons sugar, and cook until syrupy. Invert ham mixture onto serving plate; then spoon syrup over ham. Offer bread slices on the side.

• Notes •

1. Smoked ham may be substituted but there is a definite flavor difference.

2. To prepare ahead, cook ham as directed; then reheat at serving time by steaming for 20 to 30 minutes.

3. You may serve Butterfly Steamed Bread (page 176) instead of white bread.

121

Szechuan Ginger-flavored Pork

This dish is also called "fish flavored" but there is no fish in this recipe. The unique flavor of the spicy sauce is quite similar to one used with hot-braised fish, hence the association and name. Many ingredients go into this dish to make it sumptuous.

Makes: 6 to 8 servings
Cooking time: 2 hours

- 1 large tree mushroom
- 1 pound pork shoulder butt, boned and cut ⅛- by ⅛- by 1½-inches

MARINADE
- 1 tablespoon soy sauce
- 2 teaspoons dry sherry
- 2 teaspoons cornstarch
- 1 tablespoon oil

SAUCE
- 3 tablespoons soy sauce
- 1 tablespoon dry sherry
- 2 teaspoons sugar
- ½ cup chicken broth
- 1 tablespoon red rice vinegar
- 1 tablespoon cornstarch paste

    Vegetable oil, for blanching

- 2 cloves garlic, minced or pressed
- 1 teaspoon minced fresh ginger
- 1 tablespoon chili paste
- ½ cup shredded bamboo shoots
- 1 green onion, split lengthwise and cut in 1-inch pieces
- 5 water chestnuts, coarsely chopped
- ½ teaspoon sesame oil

Soak mushroom in warm water for 20 minutes; drain, remove stem, and chop.

In a bowl, combine pork with MARINADE ingredients in order listed; set aside.

Combine SAUCE ingredients and set aside.

To oil blanch, set wok over high heat for about 1 minute until hot. Add 3 to 4 cups vegetable oil and heat to 300°. Stir in pork and blanch for about 1½ minutes until redness is gone. Remove and drain.

To stir-fry, remove all but 2 tablespoons oil from wok. Stir in garlic, ginger, and chili paste; cook until fragrant. Add pork and bamboo shoots and continue stir-frying for 2 minutes. Add mushroom, green onion, and water chestnuts; stir for 30 seconds. Stir in sauce until thick. Sprinkle with sesame oil and serve.

• Notes •

1. Jicama, available in most supermarket produce sections may be substituted for water chestnuts; the flavor of both vegetables is quite similar.

2. Ginger, garlic, and green onions are very important ingredients to this dish. Make sure you cook them long enough to bring out their fragrance during stir-frying.

North China Pork

This recipe comes from a region where garlic is plentiful and even eaten as a snack, so be forewarned!

Makes: 8 servings
Cooking time: 30 minutes

1 -pound section of pork leg or butt, boned

SAUCE

5 cloves garlic, minced or pressed
1 teaspoon minced fresh ginger
1 green onion (white part), minced
1 tablespoon hot Chili Oil, page 212 or purchased
¼ cup soy sauce
2 teaspoons red rice vinegar
1 teaspoon sugar
1 teaspoon sesame oil
Salt to taste

Chinese parsley (cilantro)

To boil, place pork in enough boiling water to cover and simmer for about 20 minutes or until done. Remove, cover, and refrigerate until cool. Slice ⅛-inch thick and refrigerate until serving. Combine SAUCE ingredients well.

To serve, arrange cold pork in overlapping slices on serving platter. Pour sauce over all to serve. Garnish with parsley.

• Notes •

1. North China Pork can be served both hot and cold. If serving hot, steam slices of pork first and then top with sauce.

2. It's much easier to slice meat—especially when the recipe calls for ⅛-inch-thick slices—if it's been refrigerated or partially frozen first.

Cantonese Country Spareribs

Young and old alike enjoy these tasty pork ribs. They're perfect for a family-style dinner accompanied by a bowl of hot, steamed rice. In China, especially in Canton, you'll see them offered as dim sum in the teahouses.

Makes: 6 servings
Cooking time: 45 minutes

1 pound meaty spareribs, cut into bite-size pieces

MARINADE

1 clove garlic, minced or pressed
1 tablespoon fermented black beans, crushed
2 tablespoons soy sauce
1 tablespoon dry sherry
1 tablespoon vegetable oil
1 teaspoon sugar
1 tablespoon cornstarch
¼ teaspoon salt
1 dried red chili pod, crushed (optional)

Combine pork with MARINADE ingredients in a large bowl; mix thoroughly. Transfer to a deep footed bowl suitable for steaming.

To steam, place bowl on rack in steamer and steam over boiling water for 45 minutes. Remove and place on top of a serving platter for easier handling. Offer with rice, if desired.

• Notes •

1. Make sure the steaming bowl or plate is deep enough to hold the juices that develop during cooking.

2. You can increase the amount of chili pods for a hotter-style marinade.

3. The meatiest ribs are found on slabs weighing no more than 3 pounds.

4. If you don't have a heavy cleaver, ask your butcher to cut the ribs into pieces.

Lion's Head In Clay Pot

Yangchow, a gathering place where government officials met merchants, was a center where business was conducted over eating so some of the most elaborate dishes were created in this environment as you can well imagine. One of the most famous dishes which originated in Yangchow is Lion's Head, a delicious, succulent, and large meat patty.

Makes: 8 to 10 servings
Cooking time: 1 hour

5 to 6 dried black
mushrooms

FILLING
1½ pounds lean ground pork
10 to 12 water chestnuts,
minced
¼ package (4 oz.) bean
curd (tofu)
1 green onion (white part),
minced
2 eggs
1 teaspoon salt
1½ tablespoons cornstarch
¼ teaspoon white pepper

½ cup vegetable oil
1 head Chinese cabbage, cut
into fourths lengthwise

SEASONINGS
2 quarts Rich Chicken Broth
(page 52), or chicken
bouillon
2 thumb-size slices fresh
ginger
2 tablespoons dry sherry
Salt and white pepper to
taste

Soak mushrooms in warm water for 20 minutes; drain, remove stems, and slice.

In a large bowl, combine FILLING ingredients. Using your hands, "slap" the meat mixture against the sides of the bowl (or on a chopping block) to break down the meat. Shape into 4 large balls.

To pan-fry, set wok over medium-high heat for 1 minute. Add oil and when hot, add meatballs. Cook, for about 4 minutes or until meatballs are brown on all sides. Remove and drain.

To water-blanch, blanch cabbage sections in enough boiling water to cover for 1 minute; remove and drain. Line an 8-inch-wide earthenware clay casserole, suitable for stovetop cooking, with layers of cabbage leaves.

To cook, place meatballs on cabbage in casserole. Add enough broth to cover, mushrooms, and remaining SEASONINGS. Cover and simmer over moderate heat for 1 hour.

To serve, skim off fat and adjust seasonings. Serve in soup bowls.

• Notes •

1. Instead of "slapping" the meat to break down the tissues, you can use a food processor.

2. Instead of simmering on the stove, you can bake the casserole in a 350° oven for 1 hour.

Cucumber Cups

Cucumber cups are rarely served in restaurants because they are considered too common. This is unfortunate because they make a delicious, family-style dish—one yours will surely enjoy. By removing pork, it's an excellent vegetarian dish.

Makes: 6 servings
Cooking time: 25 minutes

2 dried black mushrooms

3 large cucumbers, all the same length

FILLING
½ pound ground pork
2 green onions (white part), minced
½ teaspoon minced fresh ginger
1 egg
½ teaspoon salt
1 teaspoon cornstarch
Dash white pepper

Soak mushroom in warm water for 20 minutes; drain, remove stem, and mince.

Lightly scrape (but do not peel) cucumbers. Cut off ends and then make decorative cuts around cucumber as illustrated below. Then cut each one into fourths. Hollow out most of the center of each section, leaving a base to form a cup. Invert on paper towels to drain. Turn back over and arrange on a wide, footed plate suitable for steaming.

Combine FILLING ingredients thoroughly. Spoon about 1 heaping tablespoon of filling in each cucumber cup.

To steam, place plate on rack in steamer and steam for 20 minutes. Remove and place on top of a serving plate for easier handling.

To serve, spoon juices over cucumber cups.

• Note •

Turn this into a vegetarian dish by substituting 2 minced black mushrooms, 1 block of bean curd (smashed), and 1 tablespoon chopped Szechuan turnips for pork in the filling.

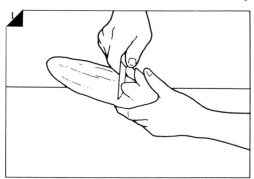

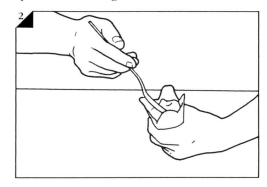

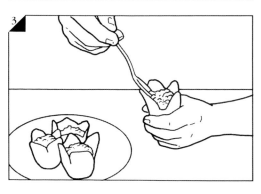

1) Decoratively cut around edge of cucumber, about ¼ of the way up from bottom. When all the way around, cut section off. (Repeat procedure 3 more times, until cucumber yields 4 decorative cups.) Cut thin, straight slice off bottom of cups to make level. 2) Hollow out center of each cup and 3) fill with 1 heaping tablespoon filling; steam.

Soochow Pearl Meatballs

These delicate pork balls are rolled in pearly sweet rice and steamed atop bok choy leaves. They are very versatile and can be served as an appetizer, with a main meal, or as a midday snack.

Makes: 16 meatballs
Cooking time: 15 minutes

1   cup sweet rice (glutinous rice)
2   dried black mushrooms

MIXTURE
½   pound lean ground pork
2   or 3 water chestnuts, coarsely chopped
1   green onion (white part), minced
½   teaspoon minced fresh ginger
1   tablespoon dry sherry
½   teaspoon sugar
½   teaspoon salt
¼   teaspoon white pepper
1   egg
1   tablespoon cornstarch

Bok choy leaves (or other greens)
Large bamboo steamer

Soak rice in warm water for 4 hours or overnight. Drain well and spread out on a plate. Soak mushrooms in warm water for 20 minutes; drain, remove stems, and mince.

Combine mushrooms and MIXTURE ingredients thoroughly in a large bowl.

To shape, grab a handful of mixture (about 4 tablespoons) and squeeze out 1-inch balls from top of fist as illustrated on page 30.

To steam, line bamboo steamer with leaves to prevent sticking. Roll meatballs in rice and place on leaves. Cover and steam over boiling water for 10 minutes. Remove and place on top of serving platter for easier handling. Bring steamer to the table to serve.

• *Notes* •

1. If possible, grind your own pork using pork butt. If you have a food processor, you can process the meat mixture at one time.

2. A bamboo steamer simplifies the serving process because you cook and serve in the same container. It's difficult to transfer hot meatballs from a conventional steamer onto a serving platter.

Orange Blossom Ribs   *Pictured on page 110, 215*

This dish is characteristic of eastern Chinese cuisine, which uses soy sauce in a method called "red cooking." Pork ribs are braised in a piquant sauce flavored with star anise, fermented red bean curd and orange juice. The redness of the sauce comes from the addition of red wine lees.

Makes: 8 to 10 servings
Cooking time: 1½ to 2 hours

- 3 pounds pork spareribs, rinsed
- 3 quarts water

RED WATER

- 9 cups water
- 5 whole star anise
- ½ cup red wine lees (red rice, page 205)
- 2 tablespoons vegetable oil

SPICES

- 3 thumb-size slices fresh ginger
- 3 green onions, cut in half
- 2 cubes red fermented bean curd

- ¼ cup soy sauce
- 2 tablespoons dry sherry
- 1 orange, quartered and seeded (or 1 cup orange juice)

- 3 ounces Chinese rock sugar or ¼ cup sugar (to taste)

Cut spareribs to separate into individual ribs.

To parboil, bring 3 quarts of water to a boil in a 14-inch wok. Add ribs and simmer briskly for 10 to 15 minutes. Remove ribs and drain.

To infuse, bring 9 cups water, star anise and red wine lees to a simmer in another pot. Simmer for 10 minutes until the red color is released. Remove from heat and pick out and reserve star anise. Strain RED WATER through a fine sieve, reserving the liquid. Discard the red wine lees.

To braise, heat 2 tablespoons oil in a Dutch oven. Add reserved star anise, ginger and green onions; stir-fry a few seconds until fragrant. Add fermented bean curd and 5 cups red water. Bring to a boil, stirring to dissolve bean cake. Add ribs and stir to coat evenly with red sauce. Add soy sauce and sherry. Squeeze orange quarters over ribs and add rinds to the pot. Return to a boil, position ribs to make sure they are submerged in liquid. Cover and briskly simmer for 30 minutes. Add rock sugar and stir until sugar is dissolved (see Notes). Add 1 cup of remaining RED WATER about every 30 minutes to keep ribs covered with liquid. Continue to simmer briskly for another 45 minutes to 1 hour, for a total cooking time of 2 hours. Watch ribs carefully to prevent burning; stir occasionally to reposition ribs and reduce heat if necessary. During the last 30 minutes, remove lid to allow sauce to reduce to a syrupy consistency with only a little sauce on the bottom of pan to glaze the ribs. The ribs should be fork-tender, soft and succulent, but still remain on the bones.

To serve, stack or arrange ribs neatly in a warm Chinese sandy clay pot or wide serving bowl.

• *Notes* •

1. This dish is better the second time around. You can prepare the ribs a day or two ahead, cover and refrigerate. Add a little water if the ribs appear dry before reheating in microwave.

2. The rock sugar is added halfway through the braising stage because sugar tends to make meat seize up and toughen when added too early.

Hunan Harvest Sauté

In Hunan province, once the harvest is over, farmers start smoking and curing meat. Smoked pork is a local speciality and a consistent ingredient in many of the provincial dishes. Here's a simple stir-fry recipe that exemplifies such a dish.

Makes: 8 servings
Cooking time: 5 minutes

1 pound smoked picnic-style ham, trimmed and sliced ¼-inch thick
2 cloves garlic, peeled and sliced
1 tablespoon fermented black beans, smashed and mixed with 1 teaspoon oil
2 leeks, washed and diagonally sliced ¼-inch thick

SAUCE
1 tablespoon soy sauce
1 teaspoon dry sherry
½ teaspoon sugar
¼ teaspoon salt

Cornstarch paste
1 teaspoon hot chili oil

To stir-fry, heat wok (or wide frying pan) over high heat for 1 minute until hot. Add ham, stir to separate, and cook for 1½ minutes. Drain off any fat. Add garlic and black bean mixture and cook until fragrant. Stir in leeks and SAUCE and toss gently. Before leeks become soggy (1½ to 2 minutes), thicken with 1 teaspoon cornstarch paste. Add hot chili oil and serve immediately.

• *Note* •
Lean, slab bacon that has been smoked could be substituted. Cut it into 1½-inch pieces for stir-frying.

BEEF & LAMB

While pork is the most plentiful meat in China, beef is the scarcest. Vast as China may be, it has very little land for grazing. Grains serve mostly as a food source for its large population, so there is not enough excess to provide feed for raising cattle. If you travel in China today, you will find excellent cuisine but few dishes on the menu feature beef. The beef dishes served may be somewhat disappointing, because the quality of beef is not comparable to American beef.

Cattle and water buffalo are considered farm laborers and have been for centuries. Milk cows are rare, since dairy products are not included in the Chinese diet. Instead, Chinese drink delicious almond or soymilk, and moisten breads not with butter but with delectable sauces and fillings made from bean or meat mixtures.

Beef dishes tend to originate from the more northern regions of cosmopolitan cities and ports, where Mongolian Beef was created to please businessmen and merchants from the West. For those who love beef, I've included luscious examples of classical Sichuan

Beef and lamb have become increasingly popular ingredients in Chinese cuisine. Gung Gung's Homestyle Oxtail Stew (page 132) will become your favorite comfort food!

cooking as well as new dishes such as Gung Gung's Homestyle Oxtail Stew, Fresh Basil Beef and Black Pepper Steak.

Buying good beef takes a good eye. Look for meat with a nice red color. If it is purplish or dark, the meat is old. If it has a yellow tinge, the meat is on the tough side or has been frozen too long. The grain should be fine-textured and firm to the touch so when a knife is inserted and removed, the meat springs back in place. *Flank steak* is excellent for all stir-fry dishes. It has less fat and gristle and is easy to trim and slice.

Stewing beef is tougher, so it is an excellent candidate for braising. The meat, gristle and fat become succulent, lending rich flavors to any dish.

Beef oxtails are an economical cut and extremely flavorful. Since it is a tougher cut, it is excellent in stews, soups, or other long-simmered dishes where braising makes it meltingly fork-tender.

I have become a fan of *lamb* on my recent travels in western China, where it is commonly eaten. Since high-quality lamb is available in America, I have added two popular lamb dishes to the menu that have become favorites with my patrons: Silk Road Lamb With Baked Sesame Buns and Wok-seared Rack of Lamb with Lemon Grass. Even those who do not usually enjoy eating lamb love these two dishes.

131

Gung Gung's Home-style Oxtail Stew

Gung Gung, my father-in-law, missed the richly flavored comfort food he grew up eating in China so we would cook this special dish in his honor. If you enjoy homemade pot roast or stew, this will surely become your favorite, too. The oxtails become soft and succulent after being braised slowly and the sauce is perfect over rice or noodles. *Pictured on page 130, 214*

Makes: 6 to 8 servings
Cooking time: 2½ to 3 hours

- 3 quarts water
- 3 pounds beef oxtails

SPICES

- 2 tablespoons vegetable oil
- 3 to 4 large ginger knobs, crushed
- 2 green onion, cut in half
- 1 celery stalk, including leaves, cut in 1-inch pieces
- ¼ medium onion, cut in 1-inch pieces
- 3 whole star anise

SAUCE

- 10 cups water
- 1 cup catsup
- ¼ cup soy sauce
- 1 to 3 tablespoons chili paste (to taste)

- 1 tablespoon vegetable oil

- 16 pearl onions, top and root end lightly trimmed, light outer skin peeled
- 16 peeled baby carrots
- 16 cherry tomatoes

Cornstarch paste

To parboil, heat 3 quarts of water to a boil in a large pot or wok. Add oxtails and parboil 15 minutes. Remove oxtails and drain. Discard water.

To stir-fry and braise, heat 2 tablespoons oil in a Dutch oven. Add ginger, green onion and celery. Stir for 1 minute. Add onion and star anise; stir-fry until onion becomes translucent. Add 6 cups water and remaining SAUCE ingredients; bring to a boil. Add oxtails and return to a boil. The liquid should cover the oxtails. If not, add a little water. Cover and briskly simmer for 30 minutes. Add one cup of water about every 30 minutes and stir occasionally to keep the meat submerged so it becomes succulent. Simmer for 2¼ to 2½ hours. Check oxtails to see if they are almost tender: the meat should be easily penetrated with a fork or chopstick, but remain on the bone.

To pan-fry, while oxtails are braising, heat 1 tablespoon oil in a small frying pan. Add pearl onions. Pan-fry until lightly browned. Add carrots and stir for 1 minute. (This can be done anytime while oxtails are braising.) After 2½ hours of braising, but before oxtails are done, transfer onions and carrots to the pot. Simmer uncovered for about 30 minutes until onions and carrots are tender and the sauce reduced. To thicken the sauce, stir in enough cornstarch paste to make a medium-consistency sauce. Add cherry tomatoes last and simmer 2 or 3 minutes to heat through. They should remain intact and not burst. Total cooking time should be about 3 hours, or until meat becomes fork-tender, silken, and succulent.

To serve, transfer stew to a large heat-proof serving bowl, clay pot or casserole. Serve with steamed rice, cooked pasta or crusty bread.

• Notes •

1. Oxtails are economical and full of flavor. You will be rewarded with a succulent stew if you don't rush the cooking process and test the meat for tenderness as it cooks.

2. This stew is tastier the second day. After cooking, cover and refrigerate. Remove fat and add a little water if needed before reheating. Make sure oxtails are thoroughly heated before serving.

Szechuan Tangerine Peel Beef

Preserved tangerine peel, with its citrus-like, almost sweet aroma and distinctive taste, transforms an ordinary stir-fried beef dish into something spectacular. We receive many requests for it at Chef Chu's.

Makes: 6 to 8 servings
Cooking time: 10 minutes

10 to 12 broken pieces preserved tangerine peel

1 pound flank steak, trimmed

MARINADE

2 teaspoons soy sauce
Pinch white pepper
2 tablespoons water
2 teaspoons cornstarch
2 tablespoons vegetable oil

Vegetable oil, for deep-frying

½ teaspoons Szechuan peppercorns
6 dried red chili pods
2 cloves garlic, sliced
2 green onions (white part), diagonally sliced ½-inch thick

SAUCE

3 tablespoons soy sauce
2 tablespoons dry sherry
1 teaspoon sugar
¼ cup chicken broth

Soak tangerine peel in warm water for 20 minutes until soft. Slice flank steak against the grain into ⅛- by 1- by 1½-inches thick. Combine with MARINADE ingredients in the order listed, mixing well after each addition. Let stand for about 10 minutes. Combine SAUCE ingredients and set aside.

To oil-blanch, set wok over high heat for about 1 minute. Add 2 cups oil and heat to 350°. Blanch beef, stirring to separate, for 2 to 3 minutes or until well done but not overcooked.

To stir-fry, remove all but 2 tablespoons oil from wok, swirling pan to coat sides. Using medium heat, stir in peppercorns quickly; then remove wok from heat for 1 minute. Remove and discard peppercorns. Return wok to heat and brown chili pods for about 30 seconds or until dark but not burnt. Add garlic and green onion, stirring for 10 seconds. Return beef along with tangerine peel and SAUCE ingredients. Cook over high heat until liquid is reduced.

Canton Oyster Beef Strips

Originating from Canton, this unique and quickly prepared dish results from stir-frying strips of marinated beef, onion, and green pepper together before blending in an oyster-flavored sauce.

Makes: 6 servings
Cooking time: 10 minutes

1 pound flank steak, trimmed

MARINADE

 2 teaspoons light or regular soy sauce
 2 tablespoons water
 1 egg white
 2 teaspoons cornstarch
 1 tablespoon vegetable oil

 1 green pepper
 ½ small white onion

SAUCE

 3 tablespoons oyster sauce
 1 tablespoon soy sauce
 1 tablespoon dry sherry
 3 tablespoons chicken broth
 ½ teaspoon sugar

 Vegetable oil, for blanching

 Cornstarch paste

Cut flank steak against the grain into 1½-inch-wide pieces; then cut with the grain into ¼-inch pieces. Finally, cut into ¼- by ¼-inch strips and then combine with MARINADE ingredients in the order listed; set aside.

Remove core and ends from bell pepper; slice lengthwise into julienne strips. Cut onion in half and then finely slice with the grain.

Combine SAUCE ingredients thoroughly; set aside.

To oil-blanch, set wok over high heat for about 1 minute. Add 3 cups oil and heat to 300°. Stir in beef, cooking just until redness is gone. Remove and drain.

To stir-fry, remove all but 3 tablespoons oil from wok. Reheat, swirling pan to coat sides. Add pepper and onion, cooking for about 1 minute until onion browns. Stir in beef and sauce, then thicken with 1 teaspoon cornstarch paste and serve.

• *Note* •

Blanched broccoli or asparagus, or sautéed green onion and ginger make a flavorful substitute for the bell pepper and onion.

Fresh Basil Beef

This dish can be served in a clay pot or oven-proof casserole. Fresh basil, garlic and chilies perfume the air and suffuses the beef with flavor.

Makes: 6 to 8 servings
Cooking time: 10 to 15 minutes

1½ pounds flank steak

2 cups cold water
1 teaspoon unseasoned meat tenderizer

MARINADE

½ teaspoon garlic powder
3 tablespoons soy sauce
2 tablespoons dry sherry
1 egg, beaten
2 tablespoons cornstarch
2 tablespoons vegetable oil

SEASONING SAUCE

¼ cup dry sherry
¼ cup soy sauce
2 tablespoons sugar (to taste)

½ cup vegetable oil for pan-searing

2 tablespoons sesame oil

SPICES

10 garlic cloves, whole or halved lengthwise
5 fresh red jalapeño chilies, seeds intact (optional), stems removed, halved lengthwise
2 stalks green onion, white part only
10 thumb-size slices of ginger

20 to 25 fresh basil leaves, stems removed
1 teaspoon Shaoxing (rice wine, page 207)

Special equipment:
One medium-size Chinese clay pot (page 209) or oven-proof covered casserole

Trim fat and gristle from steak. Slice flank steak lengthwise into 1-inch strips. Slant cut strips crosswise into 1½-inch size pieces. Pound pieces with the back of a cleaver to flatten and tenderize. Mix cold water with meat tenderizer in a large bowl. Add steak, mix well and set aside in the refrigerator for 30 minutes. Drain well.

Return steak to the bowl. Combine steak with MARINADE ingredients in the order listed; mix well after each addition. Set aside for 20 minutes. Combine the SEASONING SAUCE ingredients in another bowl. (If using a clay pot, preheat it on low to medium heat over direct flame or electric burner to prepare it for serving. Keep warm.)

To pan-sear, heat ½ cup of oil in a large wok until smoking. Lay half of the steak pieces flat in a single layer in the oil. Pan-sear for 30 seconds without turning, until golden brown. Turn once and brown the other side for 30 seconds. Remove pieces to a plate. Reheat oil and repeat pan-searing the remaining beef. Remove all oil from wok.

To stir-fry and braise, reheat wok over very high heat. Add sesame oil. Add garlic and stir-fry until golden brown and fragrant. Add remaining SPICES and stir-fry a few seconds. Return steak to wok and toss with SPICES for 30 seconds. Add one-third of the SEASONING SAUCE at a time, tossing steak vigorously for 30 seconds after each addition to reduce sauce. Add half the basil leaves and toss vigorously over high heat until the SAUCE reduces by half. The steak should be slightly pink in the middle, with a little sauce on the bottom and enough to glaze the beef.

To serve in a clay pot, immediately transfer the steak mixture to preheated clay pot. Top with remaining basil leaves and sprinkle with rice wine. Cover the pot, then place it on a heatproof platter protected with a folded, clean dry towel. Bring to the table and lift and remove lid in front of your guests. (Can be served in a heatproof covered casserole preheated in a 300° oven for 10 to 12 minutes.)

Alternately, to serve on a platter, transfer beef to a warm platter and top with fresh basil leaves. Cover platter with foil or a lid and bring to table. Lift lid or foil in front of guests. Basil should be slightly wilted and fragrant using either serving method.

• *Note* •

To make the dish hot and spicy, leave the seeds in the red jalapeños.

Silk Road Lamb With Baked Sesame Buns

I enjoyed this lamb dish along the Silk Road in China. My interpretation was a big hit when I introduced it at our Chinese New Year Banquets served with Baked Sesame Buns.

Pictured on facing page

Makes: 8 to 10 servings
Cooking time: 8 to 10 minutes

1 pound boneless leg of lamb, trimmed, fat removed, julienned ¼ x ¼ x 2-inch

MARINADE

2 tablespoons dry sherry
2 tablespoons soy sauce
1 egg
1 tablespoon cornstarch
2 tablespoons vegetable oil

2 small diameter leeks
¼ red bell pepper, seeded, julienned

SEASONING SAUCE

3 tablespoons chicken broth
3 tablespoons soy sauce
3 tablespoons dry sherry
1 teaspoon sugar
1 tablespoon cornstarch paste
6 tablespoons vegetable oil, divided

SPICES

3 jalàpeño chilies, cut in half lengthwise, seeds remain (see Notes), julienned lengthwise
2 teaspoons minced garlic cloves, thinly sliced
2 teaspoons minced fresh ginger
1 tablespoon fermented black beans, rinsed, chopped
½ teaspoon sesame oil

Baked Sesame Buns (page 177), prepared in advance

In a bowl, combine lamb with MARINADE ingredients in the order listed, mixing well after each addition. Add oil last and mix well. Set aside.

Clean the leek stalks by removing the root end and trimming the green tops to about ⅓ green part to ⅔ white. Cut stalk in half lengthwise. Separate the leaf layers under running water to rinse out any sand and grit. Slant-cut the stalk and leaves crosswise into ¾-inch lengths. Set aside with red bell pepper.

Combine SEASONING SAUCE ingredients in a bowl.

To stir-fry, heat a wok over very high heat. Add 6 tablespoons oil and heat until hot and smoking. Add lamb and stir-fry until pan-seared on the outside and rare on the inside. Remove from wok. Discard all but 3 tablespoons oil from wok. Reheat oil until very hot. Add SPICES and stir-fry 30 seconds until fragrant. Add leeks and bell pepper and stir for 1 minute until vegetables become crisp-tender. Return lamb and drizzle in SEASONING SAUCE. Toss vigorously until sauce thickens and coats everything. Stir in sesame oil last.

To serve, transfer to a serving platter. Spoon lamb into split Baked Sesame Buns and eat like a sandwich.

• Notes •

Alternative Serving Method: This dish can also be served as an entrée without the Baked Sesame Buns.

Variation: The lamb can be served inside prepared Mandarin Pancakes (page 187), warm flour tortillas, steamed buns, or on top of warm baked pizza crust, foccacia bread, or naan flatbread cut in wedges or squares.

1. Choose small-diameter leeks, found in the produce section or Asian or farmers' markets, because they tend to be more tender and firm.

2. You may substitute boneless beef top sirloin or flank steak for the lamb.

Szechuan Steamed Beef With Anise Rice

Here's a typical Szechuan dish which is served all over China. Since beef is bountiful and preferred in this country, I have suggested beef as the main ingredient; however pork or chicken are equally flavorful.

Makes: 6 to 8 servings
Cooking time: 40 minutes

SPICY RICE
- 1 cup long grain rice
- 1 star anise seed

- 1 pound flank steak (or stew beef), cut into 1½-inch cubes

MARINADE
- 1 green onion, chopped
- 1 tablespoon chili paste
- 3 tablespoons soy sauce
- 2 tablespoons dry sherry
- 3 tablespoons vegetable oil

Put rice in a bowl with enough water to cover; soak for 2 hours. Drain well and then crush (or process in food processor) with star anise. In a dry wok, toast until brown and fragrant.

Put beef in a bowl suitable for steaming. Stir in MARINADE ingredients, and rice and mix thoroughly; let stand for 10 minutes.

To steam, place bowl on rack in steamer; cover and steam over boiling water for 30 minutes. Remove and place on top of serving platter for easier handling.

• Notes •

1. If you substitute pork for beef, you'll need to steam it slightly longer to cook it completely.

2. Spicy rice mixture may be purchased at Oriental markets.

3. In China, this meat mixture is often wrapped in lotus leaves and then steamed.

4. Serves 2 if considered a single-dish meal.

Wok-seared Rack of Lamb With Lemon Grass

This exciting dish has hints of lemongrass, a subtle herb used to flavor dishes in Southeast Asia. Rack of lamb should be served rare to medium-rare to take advantage of its tender juiciness. *Pictured on page 214*

Makes: 6 to 8 servings
Cooking time: 3 to 4 minutes

2 (1 to 1¼ pounds each) racks of lamb, 7 or 8 ribs each, end bones Frenched

MARINADE

3 tablespoons water
¼ cup soy sauce
2 tablespoons dry sherry
2 tablespoons *sa cha* sauce (Chinese barbecue sauce, page 206)
2 tablespoons hoisin sauce
6 cloves garlic, peeled
1 stalk lemon grass, outer dry leaves removed, finely chopped or sliced crosswise
1 tablespoon cornstarch
2 tablespoons vegetable oil

12 stalks Chinese broccoli, ends trimmed, rinsed
3 cups chicken broth

3 to 6 tablespoons vegetable oil

Alternate presentations:
Rather than serving the lamb with the broccoli, try serving it on a ti leaf-lined platter, arranging the chops overlapping one another down the center. We often serve the lamb as an appetizer with a single chop on a lettuce leaf-lined plate garnished with cilantro or parsley.

You can French the rack of lamb yourself (remove and scrape meat and fat from the rib end bones and remove the fat over the loin), or ask your butcher do this. Cut the racks into individual chops. You should have 14 to 16 chops total. Place lamb in a bowl.

Combine MARINADE ingredients in a blender. Blend until marinade becomes smooth and the garlic and lemon grass are very finely minced. Pour marinade over the lamb and toss until well coated. Marinate lamb for at least one hour at room temperature or overnight, covered in plastic, in the refrigerator. Marinating overnight will produce more intense flavor.

To water-blanch, bring the chicken broth to a boil in a wok. Add Chinese broccoli and blanch until stalks turn bright green and crisp-tender. Remove broccoli to a colander to drain. Line stalks up parallel on cutting board. Cut stalks into three evenly sized sections about 2 inches in length. Transfer the stalks to the center of a wide platter in a neatly stacked mound, so stalks are lined up like stacked logs. Keep warm.

To wok-sear, heat a wok over high heat until it begins to smoke. Add vegetable oil and swirl to coat sides. Lay eight lamb chops in a single layer around the outside edges of the oil, with meaty side toward the center of the wok. Swirl the wok and oil around, so that the oil touches the meat and bones. Pan-sear the chops for 1½ to 2 minutes while rotating the wok slowly. Turn the lamb over to brown the other side using the same rotating motion to evenly sear the meat for about another 1½ minutes or until done to your liking. (To make sure the meat is cooked where the bone and meat come together, baste the chop with oil or rotate the pan so the oil reaches this area.) Remove lamb from wok and keep warm. Pan-sear the remaining lamb chops using additional vegetable oil as needed.

To serve, arrange lamb, bones pointing upward, with the meaty loin leaning against the Chinese broccoli in the center of the platter.

• *Notes* •

1. New Zealand lamb is available in supermarkets or from the butcher. New Zealand lamb is very tender and has small bones.

2. You may barbecue grill or use a stove-top grill to sear the lamb to desired doneness.

Black Pepper Steak

Black pepper is not used very frequently in Chinese cooking, but in this dish, it reigns supreme. Black Pepper Steak is one of the most popular items on our menu. Flank steak is tenderized to make it succulent and soft to the bite, pan-fried and seasoned with a dark flavorful sauce accented with a generous amount of black pepper, mushrooms and onions.

Makes: 10 to 12 servings
Cooking time: 5 to 7 minutes

- 2 pounds flank steak

- 2 cups cold water
- 1 teaspoon unseasoned meat tenderizer (see Notes)

MARINADE
- 1 teaspoon garlic powder
- ¼ cup soy sauce
- 2 tablespoons Shao Hsing wine
- 2 eggs, beaten
- 2 tablespoons cornstarch
- 2 tablespoons vegetable oil

SEASONING SAUCE
- ¼ cup soy sauce
- 2 tablespoons oyster sauce
- 2 tablespoons Worcestershire sauce
- 1 tablespoon Shao Hsing wine
- 1 tablespoon sugar
- 1 tablespoon cornstarch

- ¼ cup vegetable oil

- 1 tablespoon black pepper

- 24 fresh button mushrooms, sliced into 3 pieces
- 1 small yellow onion, thinly sliced lengthwise
- 2 green onions, cut into 1-inch pieces

Trim and remove gristle from steak. Cut the steak lengthwise with the grain into 1-inch strips. Slant-cut steak crosswise against the grain into 1½-inch size pieces. Pound pieces with a mallet or the back of a cleaver to flatten and tenderize. Mix cold water with meat tenderizer in a large bowl. Add steak and let soak for 1 hour, refrigerated. Drain well.

Place steak in a bowl. Add MARINADE ingredients in the order listed, mixing well after each addition. Let stand 20 minutes. Combine seasoning SAUCE ingredients in a separate bowl.

To pan-fry, heat wok over high heat until very hot. Add ¼ cup oil, swirling to coat sides. Add steak and pan-fry both sides, turning once, until browned, about 3 minutes total. Sprinkle black pepper over steak. Add mushrooms and yellow onion and green onions. Stir slowly for 1 minute, allowing mushrooms and onions to brown. Add SEASONING SAUCE and stir, for 30 seconds, until sauce thickens.

To serve, transfer to a platter. To create a dramatic sizzling presentation, pour onto a preheated cast iron platter placed on a wooden plank to protect the table.

• Notes •

1. Unseasoned meat tenderizer is a white powder found in jars in the spice section of the market. It is a dried extract from papayas called papain, which acts with liquid on meat fibers to soften them.

2. This dish is usually served on a hot cast iron platter in Chinese restaurants. The aroma and sounds will excite everyone's appetite at the table. A napkin can be loosely placed on top of the sizzling beef to prevent guests and table linens from being spattered. Remove napkin when sizzling dies down.

3. Black Pepper Steak is an ideal dish for a buffet because the larger pieces of meat are easy to serve, and the meat and flavor hold up well presented in a chafing dish or on a platter.

Mandarin Beef Stew

Here's home-style Chinese cooking at its best. It's one of the more popular items served at Chef Chu's—some customers ask for it over boiled noodles or rice, others prefer it just by itself.

Makes: 8 to 10 servings
Cooking time: 1 hour

- 2 pounds beef stew, cut into 1½-inch chunks
- 2 knobs fresh ginger, crushed
- 1 green onion, tied in a knot

In a cheesecloth bag put:
- 4 star anise seeds
- ½ teaspoon Szechuan peppercorns
- 2 pieces preserved tangerine peel
- ½ teaspoon whole cloves

- 2 tablespoons vegetable oil
- 6 to 10 whole red chili peppers
- 5 cloves garlic, slightly crushed

SEASONINGS
- ½ cup soy sauce
- 2 tablespoons dry sherry
- 2 tablespoons sugar
- 2 cups water

  Chinese parsley (cilantro)

To par-boil, place beef in enough boiling water to cover and cook for 3 minutes. Remove to colander and rinse under cold water.

In a 6-quart heavy stockpot (or earthenware pot), drop in ginger, onion, cheesecloth bag, and beef; set aside.

To stir-fry, heat wok (or wide frying pan) over high heat for 1 minute until hot. Add oil and swirl pan to coat sides. When oil is hot, add chili peppers and cook until brown. Add garlic and brown slightly. Stir in remaining SEASONINGS, and bring to a boil. Pour into stockpot and add just enough water to cover.

To stew, bring to a boil, cover, and reduce heat to medium. Cook for 45 minutes, stirring occasionally. Remove from heat and discard cheesecloth bag, ginger, and onion. Skim off any fat and garnish with Chinese parsley to serve.

• Notes •

1. I sometimes add chunks of bamboo shoots, tomato wedges, and a pinch of curry powder. Then I thicken with cornstarch paste and serve over hot boiled rice. It can also be served over boiled noodles. In either case, watch out for the chili peppers—they are hot!

2. Most Chinese prefer meat with some gristle remaining. A little gristle helps retain the shape of the meat during a long stewing time.

Szechuan Beef

Strips of marinated beef are deep-fried twice to create a light, crispy texture on the outside. Just before serving, the beef is hot-mixed in a tangy sauce made with garlic, ginger, soy sauce, and red rice vinegar then served on top of puffy rice noodles.

Makes: 6 to 8 servings
Cooking time: 15 minutes

1 pound flank steak, trimmed

MARINADE
2 teaspoons light or regular soy sauce
1 egg white
1 tablespoon cornstarch
1 tablespoon vegetable oil

BATTER
½ cup cornstarch
¼ cup water

Vegetable oil, for blanching
2 ounces rice sticks

SAUCE
5 tablespoons soy sauce
¼ cup water or chicken broth
1 tablespoon red rice vinegar
1 tablespoon sugar

½ teaspoon minced fresh ginger
1 large clove garlic, minced or pressed

Cornstarch paste
1½ teaspoons hot chili oil
½ teaspoon sesame oil
1 green onion (including top), chopped

Cut flank steak against the grain into ¼- by 1- by 1½-inch-thick slices. Combine with MARINADE ingredients in the order listed, mixing well. Let stand for 10 minutes.

Combine cornstarch and water to make a paste; set aside.

To deep-fry, heat 4 cups oil in a wok (or electric deep-fat fryer) to 350°. Add rice sticks and deep-fry for about 30 seconds until puffy. Remove, break into small pieces and arrange on serving platter. Remove any pieces left in oil and then return oil to 350°. Dip beef slices, a few at a time, into cornstarch paste and then deep-fry in oil until a hard crust is formed. Remove, drain, and keep oil warm. Skim oil for any leftover crus and discard.

Combine SAUCE ingredients thoroughly; set aside.

To deep-fry again, bring oil back to 350°. Add beef all at once and fry for about 1 minute until hard crust forms again. Remove and drain.

To hot mix, remove all but 3 tablespoons oil from wok. Add ginger and garlic, cooking until fragrant. Stir in sauce, bring to a boil, and thicken with 1 tablespoon cornstarch paste until the consistency of syrup is reached. Sprinkle with chili oil and sesame oil. Return beef to wok and toss with green onion. Mix well and serve on top of rice sticks.

To serve, toss beef with rice sticks at the table.

• *Notes* •

1. "Hot mixing" is just that—quickly mixing crisp, deep-fried or cooked ingredients with a sauce. It's intended to mix the ingredients not cook them any more.

2. This recipe is ideal for entertaining because everything, except for the hot mixing, can be done in advance.

Mongolian Beef

In Mongolia, cattle herders move with their cattle across the open range like American cowboys once did. They cook their meals over an open fire, using ingredients on hand or seasonings that transport easily. This beef dish, cooked the same way over hot, direct heat, uses just a few basic seasonings for flavor.

Makes: 4 to 6 servings
Cooking time: 10 minutes

1 pound flank steak, trimmed

MARINADE

2 teaspoons light or regular soy sauce
2 tablespoons water
Pinch white pepper
2 teaspoons cornstarch
2 tablespoons vegetable oil

1 bunch green onions

SAUCE

3 tablespoons soy sauce
1 tablespoons dry sherry
1 teaspoon sugar

¼ cup vegetable oil
10 thumb-size slices fresh ginger

Cornstarch paste

Cut flank steak against the grain into ⅛- by 1- by 1½-inch slices. Then combine with MARINADE ingredients in the order listed; mix well and set aside.

Cut onions into 1½-inch-long pieces, then separate outer layers from inner ones.

Combine SAUCE ingredients; set aside.

To stir-fry, set wok (or wide frying pan) over high heat for 1 minute until hot. Add oil and swirl pan to coat sides. When oil is very hot, add beef, stirring to distribute evenly in pan and to sear both sides. Add ginger, stirring until fragrant. Add green onion; mix well and stir for 30 seconds. Pour in sauce, stir-fry quickly until green onion starts to wilt. Slightly thicken with 1 teaspoon cornstarch paste and serve.

• *Note* •

This kind of stir-frying must be done over high heat for only a short period of time to bring out the flavor of the ingredients.

VEGETABLES

America is a bountiful country, rich in high-quality meats and produce, and, with the great influx of Asian immigrants, the variety of vegetables found in supermarkets and Asian grocery stores is beginning to match the variety found in China. Some of the most popular are snow peas, *bok choy*, napa cabbage, mustard greens, Chinese broccoli, *ong choy*, *yu choy*, Chinese okra *sin gua*, long beans, hot chili peppers, pea shoots, lemon grass, bean sprouts, yellow and green garlic chives, and Asian eggplants. Tofu or bean curd of many kinds may also be found in most supermarkets, along with dried and fresh shiitake (black forest) mushrooms, canned bamboo shoots, dried lily roots, and many other vegetables described in the Asian Ingredients section (pages 200–207).

Chinese cooking brings out the flavor of vegetables through very light cooking methods. In some cases, vegetables are water- or broth-blanched first to lightly pre-cook them, add flavor and lessen final cooking time.

Vegetables are the mainstay of Chinese cooking, available year-round and grown in home gardens and on large farms. Crispy Tofu Bites (page 36), Szechuan Pickled Cucumber Spirals (page 37), Szechuan-style String Beans (page 147), and Braised Eggplant (page 155) can be served as appetizers or entrees.

Although bean curd, or bean cake, does not look like a vegetable, it is made from pureed soy beans combined with a coagulant similar to that added to make cheese, then pressed into blocks about 3 inches square. Tofu is a staple in Chinese cuisine because it is high in protein, inexpensive, and absorbs all the flavors when cooked in a delicious sauce. If you want to make healthier eating choices, you might consider incorporating bean curd into your diet— it is easy to digest and low in calories. For a satisfying combination, add several half-inch cubes or slices of bean curd to Rich Chicken Broth and you'll have a nutritious, light soup.

Vegetarians can satisfy their taste buds thoroughly with Chinese cooking. Buddhists and Taoists are strictly vegetarian and because their philosophy is highly regarded throughout China, many of their delicious vegetarian specialties are considered classic Chinese cuisine. So much so that Chinese honor and celebrate the New Year by serving one of their delectable dishes. In many recipes that appear in the other sections of the book, tofu or additional vegetables may be served in place of the meat. You may use vegetable broth in any dish or soup that calls for chicken broth without compromising the flavor of the dish. And the small amount of meat used in some vegetable dishes is used to add flavor, but may be omitted if you prefer.

Stir-fried Bean Sprouts

A simple dish with a simple taste, this is easy on the budget and quick to prepare. Timing is critical.

Makes: 6 to 8 servings
Cooking time: 5 minutes

- 3 tablespoons vegetable oil
- 6 to 8 dried chili pods (optional)
- 2 green onions, cut into 1½-inch pieces
- 3 thumb-size slices fresh ginger, slivered
- 4 cups bean sprouts
- ½ teaspoon salt
- 2 teaspoons sugar
- 1 teaspoon white vinegar

To stir-fry, heat wok (or wide frying pan) over high heat for 1 minute until hot. Add oil and swirl pan to coat sides. Stir in chili pods (if used), cooking just until brown. Add green onions and ginger, stir-frying for 10 seconds. Add bean sprouts, quickly stirring over maximum heat, for 30 seconds. Mix in salt, sugar, and vinegar. Toss vigorously about 45 seconds (to prevent bean sprouts from wilting). Quickly remove to serving platter.

• *Notes* •

1. To add hotness to this dish, break open one or more chili pods to expose seeds. Remember, the more you break open the hotter the dish will be!

2. Use maximum heat for stir-frying. You're trying to force the flavor out yet keep the texture crunchy.

Snow Peas With Water Chestnuts   *Pictured on page 80*

Jade green snow peas and coin-like slices of water chestnuts make this the most requested Chinese vegetable combination in America.

Makes: 6 to 8 servings
Cooking time: 5 minutes

- 1 can (8 oz.) sliced water chestnuts
- 2 cups snow peas, ends trimmed

SAUCE
- ½ cup Rich Chicken Broth (page 52), or chicken bouillon
- ½ cube chicken bouillon
- 2 tablespoons dry sherry
- ½ teaspoon sugar
  Salt to taste
  Pinch white pepper

- 3 tablespoons vegetable oil
- 1 green onion (white part), minced

  Cornstarch paste

To water-blanch, cook water chestnuts and snow peas in boiling water for 30 seconds. Remove and drain.
   Combine SAUCE ingredients; set aside.
   To stir-fry, heat wok (or wide frying pan) over high heat for 1 minute until hot. Add oil and swirl pan to coat sides. When oil is hot, add onion and cook until fragrant. Stir in sauce and vegetables to coat. Thicken with 2 tablespoons cornstarch paste and transfer to serving platter.

Lettuce With Oyster Sauce

What can you serve on the spur of the moment when someone unexpected arrives for dinner? Try cooking lettuce. This is unusual, quick, and never fails to win approval.

Makes: 6 servings
Cooking time: 5 minutes

1 head Romaine lettuce

SAUCE
¼ cup oyster sauce
2 tablespoons vegetable oil
1 tablespoon sesame oil

Immerse lettuce in cold water for 5 minutes; then cut off stem end.

To water-blanch, cook lettuce in boiling water for 30 seconds. Remove and drain; cut into thirds crosswise and place on serving platter.

Combine SAUCE ingredients and spoon over lettuce. Toss gently at the table to serve.

• Note •

Why not use asparagus, broccoli, or another vegetable you have on hand instead of lettuce? You'll need to blanch them about 2 minutes.

Szechuan-style String Beans

Typically, this recipe is saved for the restaurant or professional kitchens in China because for maximum flavor you need intense heat. However, I've developed a technique for this "dry" stir-frying process that can be successfully duplicated at home.

Makes: 6 to 8 servings
Cooking time: 5 minutes

1 tablespoon dried shrimp

Vegetable oil, for blanching

1 pound string beans, trimmed and cut into 2-inch lengths
1 ounce ground pork
1 clove garlic, minced or pressed
1 teaspoon minced preserved Szechuan mustard green
1 teaspoon chili paste

SEASONINGS
1 tablespoon dry sherry
2 tablespoons soy sauce
3 tablespoons chicken broth
¼ teaspoon sugar

Soak shrimp in warm water for 5 to 10 minutes; drain and mince.

To oil-blanch, set wok over high heat for about 1 minute. Add 2 to 3 cups oil and heat to 350°. Blanch beans in batches for about 1½ minutes or until wrinkles form. Remove and drain.

To stir-fry, remove all but 3 tablespoons oil. Reheat wok until hot. Add pork, stirring to separate. Add garlic, mustard green, shrimp, and chili paste. Stir-fry for 30 seconds; return beans to wok and then stir in SEASONINGS. Toss gently until liquid coats string beans. Remove and serve immediately.

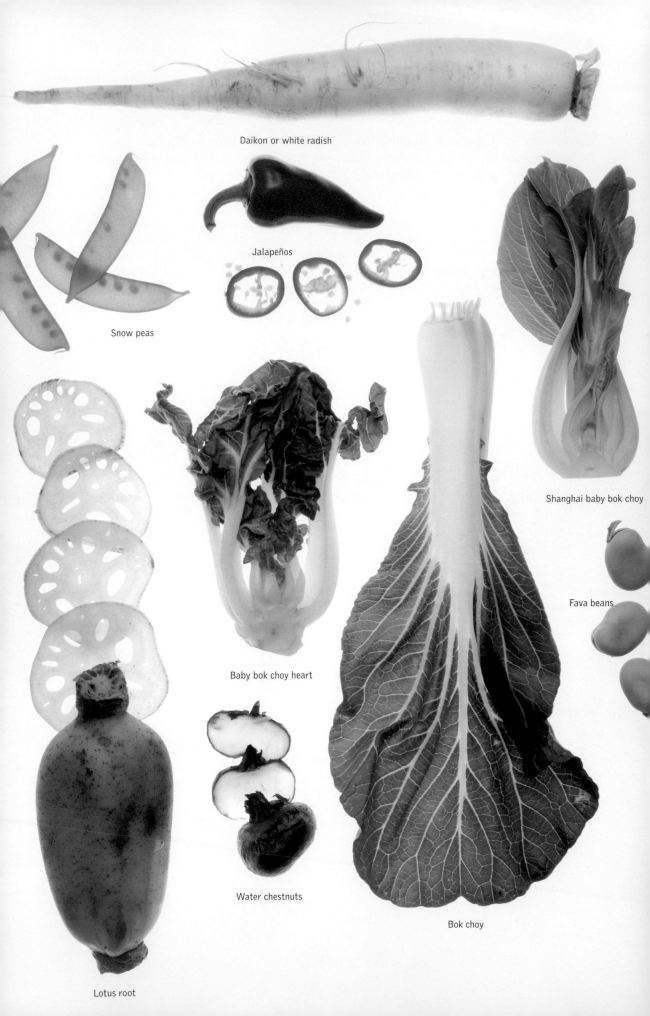

Daikon or white radish

Jalapeños

Snow peas

Shanghai baby bok choy

Fava beans

Baby bok choy heart

Lotus root

Water chestnuts

Bok choy

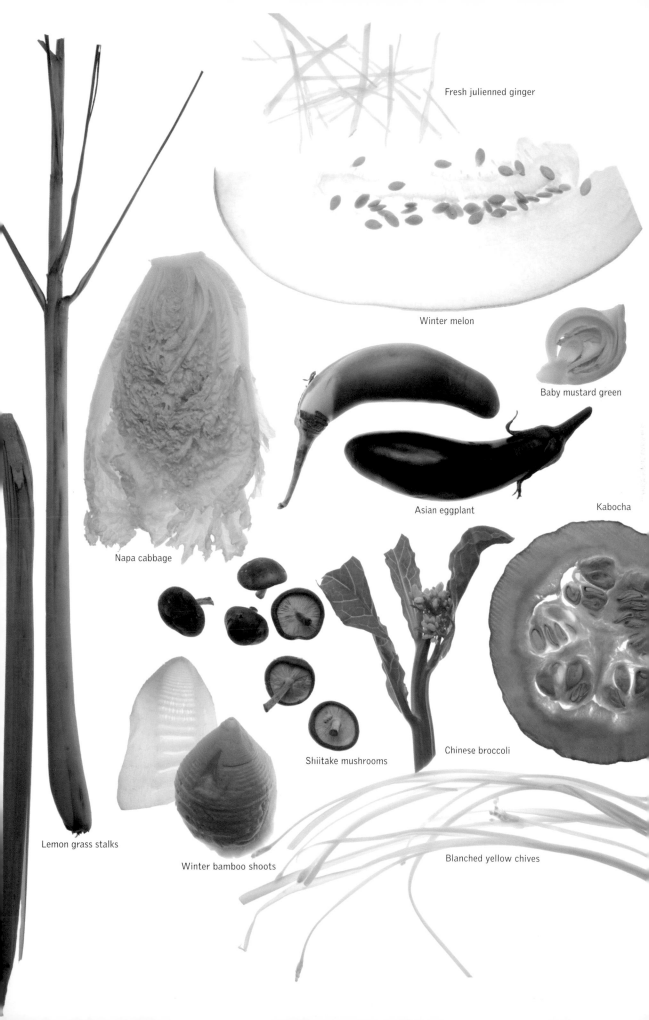

Fresh julienned ginger

Winter melon

Baby mustard green

Napa cabbage

Asian eggplant

Kabocha

Shiitake mushrooms

Chinese broccoli

Lemon grass stalks

Winter bamboo shoots

Blanched yellow chives

Mixed Chinese Vegetables

Just like any other dish that relies on the choicest ingredients, this recipe requires a little extra time when selecting the vegetables. Look for ones at their peak of freshness with good color and texture.

Makes: 8 servings
Cooking time: 10 minutes

4 or 5 dried black
   mushrooms

VEGETABLES
½ small head broccoli
2 or 3 stalks bok choy,
   slant-cut into 1½-inch
   pieces
¼ cup sliced water chestnuts
¼ cup sliced bamboo shoots
12 snow peas, ends trimmed
12 canned baby corn
8 to 12 canned straw
   mushrooms

SEASONINGS
½ cup chicken broth
½ teaspoon dry sherry
1 teaspoon salt
½ teaspoon sugar
   Pinch white pepper

3 tablespoons vegetable oil
1 green onion (white part),
   minced
1 thumb-size slice fresh
   ginger, minced

   Cornstarch paste

Soak mushrooms in warm water for 20 minutes; drain, remove stems, and cut in half. Cut broccoli flowerets into bite-size pieces; slice stems ⅛-inch thick.

To water-blanch, cook broccoli, bok choy, and black mushrooms in boiling water for 1 minute; add remaining VEGETABLES and blanch for 30 seconds. Remove and drain.

Combine SEASONINGS together; set aside.

To stir-fry, heat wok (or wide frying pan) over high heat for 1 minute until hot. Add oil and swirl pan to coat sides. When oil is hot, add green onion and ginger, stirring until fragrant. Stir in seasonings, add vegetables, and stir-fry for 1½ minutes. Thicken with 2 teaspoons cornstarch paste and serve.

• Notes •

1. Rendered chicken fat is often used in China to enrich the flavor of this vegetable dish. Use a few drops after thickening sauce with cornstarch paste.

2. Almost any vegetable dish—snow peas with water chestnuts, black mushrooms, or Chinese greens—may be prepared in this manner.

3. Vegetarians can substitute vegetable bouillon for chicken broth.

Shanghai Braised Three Delicacies

Here's a tasty Shanghai-style dish that is perfect for vegetarians. The taste is wonderful because the deep-fried gluten puffs absorb all the other flavors during braising.

Makes: 6 to 8 servings
Cooking time: 30 minutes

- 5 to 7 dried black mushrooms
- 1 can (15 oz.) winter bamboo shoots
- 1 package (1 lb.) frozen gluten puff, thawed and torn into 1-inch pieces

  Vegetable oil, for deep-frying

- 1 tablespoon vegetable oil
- 1 thumb-size chunk fresh ginger, crushed
- 3 green onions (white part), diagonally sliced ½-inch thick

SEASONINGS

- 3 cups Rich Chicken Broth (page 52), or vegetable bouillon
- 5 tablespoons soy sauce
- 1 tablespoon dry sherry
- 2 tablespoons sugar
- ½ teaspoon salt

- 1 teaspoon sesame oil

Soak mushrooms in warm water for 20 minutes; drain, remove stems, and cut into bite-size pieces. Cut bamboo shoots into bite-size pieces using rolling-cut method (see page 195).

To boil, bring puffs to boil in 2 quarts water for 5 minutes. Remove and drain, squeezing out excess water. Let dry for about 5 minutes.

To deep-fry, heat 4 cups oil in a wok (or electric deep-fat fryer) to 350°. Add gluten puffs in two batches. Deep-fry for 8 to 10 minutes or until golden brown; outside should be firm and all the moisture should be gone. Remove and drain well. Add bamboo shoots to oil and fry for about 3 minutes; remove and drain.

To braise, remove all but 1 tablespoon oil and return wok to heat for 1 minute; swirl pan to coat sides. Stir in ginger and onion, cooking until fragrant. Add gluten puffs, bamboo shoots, mushrooms, and SEASONINGS. Braise over medium heat, stirring occasionally, for about 10 minutes or until most of the liquid is absorbed. Stir in sesame oil and discard ginger before serving.

• Notes •

1. Frozen gluten puff is available at Oriental markets.

2. We deep-fry them first to achieve a sponge-like texture outside; then we braise them to absorb all the flavor. (For more information, see page 204.)

3. This dish may be served hot or cold. It can be made ahead and refrigerated until serving; while reheating, add a few snow peas for color.

Hunan Village Tofu   *Pictured on facing page*

Hunan Village Tofu is a popular dish on the restaurant menu as well as at Chinese banquets. It even wins fans from those who think they don't like tofu. We use soft tofu which has a smooth custard-like texture and forms a mild contrast to the bold, tantalizing flavors of smoked ham, chilies and fermented black beans, which give this dish its character and taste.

Makes: 6 to 8 servings
Cooking time: 10 to 15 minutes

- 2 pounds soft tofu, drained and patted dry

SAUCE

- 1 cup vegetable or chicken broth
- 3 tablespoons soy sauce
- 1 teaspoon sugar
- 1 quart vegetable oil

SPICES

- 2 jalapeño chilies, thinly sliced
- 6 cloves garlic, peeled and thinly sliced
- 2 ounces smoked ham, finely shredded (for vegetarian style, see Notes)
- 3 tablespoons fermented black beans, rinsed and chopped
- 3 green onions, cut into 1-inch pieces
- 1 teaspoon sesame oil
- 1 tablespoon cornstarch paste

Carefully place each tofu block on the cutting board. Cut each tofu block vertically crosswise and lengthwise in half making 4 quarters each. Cut each quarter crosswise into 3 equal pieces, making 12 pieces from each block, or 24 total. Soft tofu is very fragile. Transfer pieces supported by the side of your cleaver. Combine SAUCE ingredients in a bowl.

To deep-fry, heat 3 cups of oil in a wok to 375°. Gently place 6 pieces of tofu into the wok, without breaking them. Fry for about 1 minute to form a light crust; remove carefully with a spatula or wire strainer and drain. Repeat with remaining pieces. Maintain a high oil temperature to create a crust outside which will keep the tofu pieces from breaking apart.

To braise, remove all oil from wok except 2 tablespoons. Reheat oil; add chilies and garlic and stir a few seconds until fragrant. Add remaining SPICES and stir-fry for 30 seconds. Stir in SAUCE and bring to a boil. Gently return tofu to wok and braise gently for 30 seconds. Add green onions and sesame oil. Thicken sauce with cornstarch paste to a light sauce consistency, stirring very gently. Transfer to a serving platter.

• Notes •

1. **Alternative Cooking Method:** Pan-fry tofu in a skillet with $1/4$ inch of hot, preheated oil on the bottom. Brown both sides well, turning tofu carefully. Remove and drain.

2. Maintaining tofu shape is a part of the character of this dish. Try to keep the tofu pieces from breaking apart when you handle them.

3. For vegetarian style, omit the smoked ham and use vegetable broth instead of chicken broth in the sauce.

Tientsin Cabbage

The natural, light sweet flavor of cabbage makes this dish, enhanced by a shrimp topping. Most Chinese vegetables are cooked quickly to preserve their crunchy texture. This recipe results in very soft cabbage ready to melt in your mouth.

Makes: 6 to 8 servings
Cooking time: 25 minutes

10 dried shrimp

 2 small heads Chinese
    cabbage
½ teaspoon salt
 1 cup chicken broth

 2 tablespoons vegetable oil
    Salt to taste
    Pinch white pepper
    Cornstarch paste

Soak shrimp in warm water for 30 minutes; remove, drain, and mince. Cut off tops and ends of cabbage; then cut into eighths lengthwise.

To par-boil, place cabbage in enough boiling water to cover and cook for 10 minutes or until soft. Remove, run under cold water, and drain.

To assemble, arrange cabbage sections decoratively in a medium-size bowl suitable for steaming. Sprinkle salt over cabbage; then sprinkle shrimp. Carefully pour in broth.

To steam, place bowl on rack in steamer. Cover and steam over boiling water for 10 minutes; carefully drain broth into another bowl and reserve. Invert cabbage onto serving platter, flattening down slightly.

To cook, heat wok over high heat; add oil, swirling pan to coat sides. Pour in reserved broth (including shrimp) and bring to a boil. Season to taste with salt and pepper; then thicken with 4 teaspoons cornstarch paste.

To serve, spoon sauce over cabbage sections.

• *Notes* •

1. Dried scallops—soaked in boiling water for 30 minutes and then slivered—can be used instead of shrimp, if desired.

2. Try assembling cabbage sections in overlapping rows similar to Hunan Honey-glazed Ham, pictured on page 120.

Braised Eggplant

Deep-purple Oriental eggplant, available at some supermarkets as well as most Oriental markets, are preferred for this recipe. Their skin is so tender, peeling isn't necessary. Besides eggplant, you'll discover an assortment of tasty ingredients: ground pork, water chestnuts, ginger, garlic, green onion, and chili paste.

Makes: 6 servings
Cooking time: 10 minutes

8 Oriental eggplant, cut in half lengthwise and then into two sections

SAUCE

3 tablespoons soy sauce
1 tablespoons sugar
1 cup Rich Chicken Broth (page 52), or chicken bouillon
1 tablespoon dry sherry
¼ teaspoon salt

Vegetable oil, for deep-frying

2 ounces ground pork

SPICES

2 cloves garlic, minced or pressed
1 teaspoon minced fresh ginger
1 tablespoon chili paste

2 tablespoons coarsely chopped water chestnuts (or jicama)
1 tablespoon red rice vinegar
1 green onion (including top), coarsely chopped

Cornstarch paste
1 teaspoon sesame oil

Score each section of eggplant, cutting into fan-shaped pieces as pictured on page 149.

Combine SAUCE ingredients; set aside.

To deep-fry, heat 2 cups oil in a wok to 350°. Drop in eggplant pieces, a few at a time, and deep-fry for about 3 minutes or until soft. Remove and drain well.

To braise, remove all but 1 tablespoon oil from wok. Reheat oil until hot and then add pork, stirring to separate. Add garlic, ginger, and chili paste; stir-fry until fragrant. Return eggplant to wok along with water chestnuts and sauce. Braise over medium heat until liquid is reduced; then add vinegar and green onion. Mix thoroughly and thicken slightly with 1 tablespoon cornstarch paste. Stir in sesame oil and serve.

• Notes •

1. You can leave the skin on the eggplant as directed, or you can score the skin making slashes ¹⁄₁₆-inch apart for a more decorative look.

2. Make sure to drain the eggplant well after deep-frying so that it won't taste greasy.

3. Vegetarians can enjoy this dish by simply deleting the pork.

Four Seasons Vegetables

Presentation is the key to the success of this elegant dish. The vegetables star, so choose the very freshest.

Makes: 6 to 8 servings
Cooking time: 10 minutes

VEGETABLES

- 12 dried black mushrooms
- 4 firm red tomatoes
- 1 head broccoli
- 24 canned baby corn, drained

- 1 quart Rich Chicken Broth (page 52), or chicken bouillon

SEASONINGS

- ½ cube chicken bouillon
  Salt to taste
  Dash white pepper

  Cornstarch paste
- 1 tablespoon vegetable oil

Soak mushrooms in warm water for 20 minutes; drain, remove stems, and cut mushrooms in half. Cut 3 slices (½-inch wide) from sides of tomatoes, cutting from top to bottom. (You should have a triangular-shaped tomato "core" left; reserve for other uses.)

Remove broccoli stalks (save for other uses); slice flowerets in half lengthwise.

To water-blanch, bring broth to a boil. Add black mushrooms, cook for about 3 minutes, and remove. Add broccoli, cook for 3 minutes, remove, and drain. Blanch tomatoes, and baby corn separately in boiling broth for 1 minute; remove and drain. Plunge tomatoes in cold water to cool; then peel off skin. Pour 2 cups broth through strainer into a wok (discarding seeds).

To assemble, arrange vegetables attractively on a white serving platter.

To cook, bring broth to a boil with SEASONINGS. Thicken with 2 tablespoons cornstarch paste; then stir in oil. Ladle over vegetables to serve.

• Notes •

1. You can substitute other vegetables for those suggested above but retain the 4 different colors. (For example, substitute white asparagus for corn, bok choy or asparagus for broccoli.)

2. Save the chicken broth for other uses; first remove any leftover vegetable pieces using a strainer.

3. I use the reserved tomato cores in other dishes like Egg Flower Soup (page 59).

Ma Po's Hot Bean Curd

Chinese say that a long time ago a woman known as Lady "Pock-mark" made this dish famous throughout the Szechuan province. I'm not sure what her name has to do with it, but her recipe is typically Szechuan—hot enough to stimulate the palate and numb the tongue.

Makes: 6 to 8 servings
Cooking time: 10 minutes

1 block (16 oz.) soft bean curd (tofu)

SAUCE
1 cup Rich Chicken Broth (page 52), or chicken bouillon
3 tablespoons soy sauce
1 tablespoon dry sherry
2 teaspoons sugar
½ teaspoon salt

3 tablespoons vegetable oil
2 ounces ground pork (or beef)
1 clove garlic, minced or pressed
2 teaspoons chili paste

1 green onion, chopped
Cornstarch paste

1 teaspoon hot chili oil (optional)
½ teaspoon sesame oil
Pinch ground roasted Szechuan peppercorns

Cut soft bean curd into ½-inch cubes.

Combine SAUCE ingredients; set aside.

To braise, set wok over high heat for 1 minute until hot. Add oil and swirl pan to coat sides. Add pork, stirring to separate. Add garlic and chili paste, stirring for 30 seconds until fragrant. Pour in sauce and bean cake. Bring to a boil and braise for 5 minutes. Stir in green onion for 30 seconds, then thicken with 1½ tablespoons cornstarch paste. Mix in chili and sesame oil, remove to a serving plate, sprinkle with peppercorns, and mix to serve.

• *Notes* •

1. To make a vegetarian dish, substitute presoaked sliced black mushrooms for the pork.

2. Make sure the seasoning spices and the bean cake are blended together well. The bean cake should be hot (temperature-wise), saltier than normal, and spicy hot with an aromatic flavor.

3. It's nice to accompany with steamed rice.

EGGS, NOODLES & RICE

Eggs, such simple things, have been converted by the Chinese into many tastes. I know of no cuisine in which the egg plays such a varied role—from "thousand-year-old" eggs, to salted duck eggs, to marbled chicken eggs, to dainty quail eggs. Chinese also cook eggs by the more standard methods of shirring, baking, steaming, pan-frying, and deep-frying. Entire cookbooks have been devoted to eggs cooked Chinese-style, and I regret that we have space only for a few of my very favorite egg recipes.

Noodles may be part of a Chinese family's daily diet, but they perform an auspicious duty as well. Because they are cut in long strands, noodles have been, for centuries, symbolic of long life. Noodles are always served for birthdays, New Year's and other festive occasions. It is believed that all who partake in eating these celebration noodles share in the blessing. Noodles may be eaten as a snack, as part of a meal (as one of the last courses in a banquet), or as a meal itself. Our Pan-fried Angel-Hair Noodles is the perfect example of a one-dish meal that is a

delectable combination of ingredients, flavors and textures.

Rice is a staple in China and is generally eaten three times a day, at all meals. It is often omitted in formal or banquet meals because it is such "common" food. If it does appear at a banquet, it is served at the end of the meal, so the guests understand that they are not expected to "fill up" on rice, but on the more elaborate dishes. There are three basic types of rice. Glutinous (or sweet) rice is short-grained, milky white, and becomes sticky when cooked. Our savory recipe for Taiwan Aboriginal Sticky Rice will delight sticky-rice lovers. Glutinous rice is also an essential ingredient for stuffings, pastries, and desserts, such as Eight Treasure Rice Pudding. Long-grain white rice is the variety most commonly used in Chinese cooking and is fluffy when steamed. Short-grain rice, commonly used in Japanese cooking, is a bit starchy and is used to make our homey Congee. Brown rice is becoming popular again because of its improved health benefits and nutrition. Mixed-rice combinations, basmati and jasmine rice are also available in supermarkets and Asian groceries and offer a variety of tastes, aromas and textures to round out a meal. The Chinese expression for let's go and eat is, "let's go and eat rice!"

Timing and careful attention are crucial in the preparation of fresh noodles. Pan-fried Angel Hair Noodles (page 170) are a Hong Kong favorite.

Marble Eggs *Pictured on facing page*

The unusual appearance of these eggs—fine dark lines in a pattern similar to marble—makes them an impressive addition to any appetizer or cold plate selection. Chinese also enjoy them as a simple accompaniment to rice porridge or *congee.*

Makes: 6 servings
Cooking time: 1½ hours

12 eggs
2 quarts water

SEASONINGS

3 bags black tea (or 3 tablespoons loose black tea leaves)
3 tablespoons soy sauce
2 teaspoons Chinese five-spice
2 star anise
1 green onion, tied in a knot
1 thumb-size slice fresh ginger

Shredded lettuce

Place eggs in a large pot, cover with cold water, and bring to a simmer. Simmer for about 15 minutes, rinse and drain, and let cool. Gently crack shells, but do not remove until a pattern of fine cracks appear all over.

To simmer, return cracked eggs to the pot, add the 2 quarts of water, and stir in SEASONINGS. Bring to a boil, reduce heat, and simmer for about 1 hour. Remove from heat and allow eggs to cool completely in the liquid.

To serve, shell eggs and slice or cut into quarters; or if you prefer, leave eggs whole. Place on a bed of lettuce to serve.

• *Notes* •

1. Chinese most often serve Marble Eggs in sections, presented as part of a cold plate.
2. Try bringing these fanciful eggs on your next picnic.

Fresh Noodles & Wrappers

Here's an all-purpose noodle recipe that can easily be adapted to making fresh egg roll and won-ton wrappers, too.

Makes: 6 to 8 servings
Cooking time: 15 minutes

2 cups all-purpose flour
1 egg, lightly beaten
¼ cup water
Pinch salt

1 cup cornstarch
1 cloth handkerchief (to wrap around cornstarch)

2 quarts water
3 cups cold water
2 tablespoons vegetable oil

Mound flour in a large mixing bowl or on a work surface. Make a deep well in the center and pour in egg, water, and salt. Using a chopstick or fork, mix ingredients well and then knead dough into a stiff ball. Cover with a damp cloth and let stand for 10 minutes.

Meanwhile, spoon cornstarch into the center of the handkerchief. Holding all 4 corners, shake cornstarch down into a "bag" and tie securely with string. Set aside.

To shape, knead dough by hand for 4 to 5 minutes, dusting the board and dough with cornstarch bag to prevent sticking. Using a rolling pin, roll dough out into a rectangle about ⅛-inch thick.

Roll up rectangle evenly onto the rolling pin as illustrated, pressing down firmly and evenly to further stretch the dough. Unroll the dough, dust with cornstarch on both sides, and roll up on rolling pin again (change the position so that all the dough remains about the same thickness). Repeat this procedure until the dough is 1/16-inch thick all over.

To cut, unroll the dough for the last time by unfolding it in such a way that pleats are created (see illustration). The pleats should be about 2 inches wide. Using a sharp cleaver or knife, slice straight across the folds, making strips 1/16-inch wide. Cut all the way through and cut the entire length of the dough. Carefully lift up the top layer (pleat) of noodles and unfold.

To cook, bring 2 quarts water to a boil in a large pot. Add noodles, stirring to separate, and return to a boil. Pour in cold water, then bring to a boil again. Remove and pour noodles through a colander; rinse under cold water and drain well. Mix with oil to serve.

Variation: Egg Roll Wrappers and **Won-ton Wrappers.** Follow the same procedure for making noodles and roll out as directed until a thickness of 1/16-inch is reached. Using a ruler and a sharp cleaver or knife, cut dough into 7-inch squares for egg roll wrappers or 3½-inch squares for won-ton wrappers. Dust with cornstarch and then stack them; wrap in plastic until ready to use.

Making & Cutting Fresh Noodles

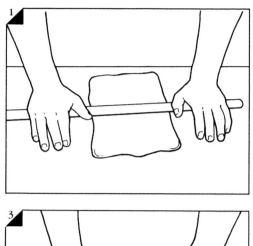

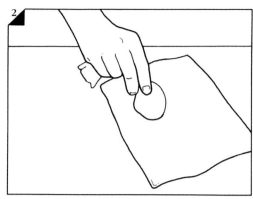

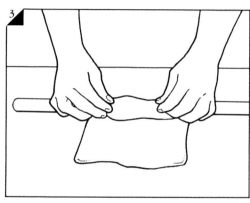

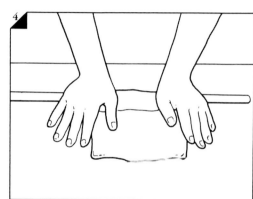

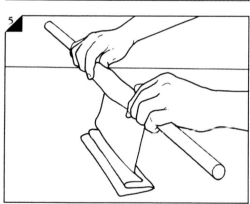

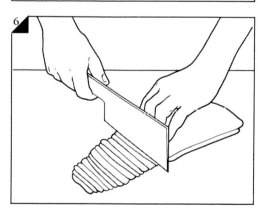

1) Roll out dough into a rectangle, 2) dusting dough with cornstarch bag. 3) Roll dough up evenly onto rolling pin, 4) pressing down firmly and evenly as you go to further stretch dough. Unroll dough, dust with cornstarch on both sides, and roll up again; repeat procedure until dough is 1/16-inch thick. 5) Unroll dough for the last time by unfolding it in pleats. Using a sharp knife, 6) slice across folds at one end, making strips about 1/16-inch wide. Cut entire length of dough this way and 2) lift up top layer (pleat) and unfold noodles.

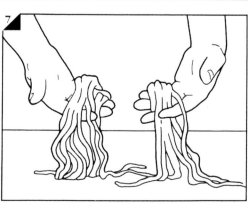

Taiwan Aboriginal Sticky Rice   *Pictured on facing page*

This popular rice dish can contain a range of ingredients to suit your taste. The rice is served al dente so it is less sticky than most glutinous rice dishes. For an authentic presentation, wrap it in bamboo leaves or a lotus leaf.

Makes: 6 to 8 servings
Cooking time: 1 hour

- 2 cups glutinous rice, rinsed
- 6 ounces pork butt, cut in ¼- by 1½- inch strips

MARINADE
- 1 teaspoon soy sauce
- ¼ teaspoon cornstarch
- 2 teaspoons vegetable oil
- 2 tablespoons vegetable oil
- 1 tablespoon thinly sliced dried shallots
- 6 dried black mushrooms, reconstituted, stems removed, shredded
- ¼ cup chicken broth
- 1 tablespoon soy sauce
- ½ teaspoon salt
- ⅛ teaspoon white pepper
- 2 dried lotus leaves

GARNISH
- Chinese parsley (cilantro), chopped
- Dried fried shallots
- *Xuan chi* pickles, julienned or diced

• Notes •

Hint: Aboriginal rice is usually served al dente, where the rice grains are separate. If you like your rice softer or stickier, steam the rice a little longer.

1. Taiwanese or Cantonese *lop cheong* sausage can be used in place of the pork. You may add some finely diced carrot and onion for color. Other additions include seeded dried red dates, winter bamboo shoots, canned gingko nuts, raisins or dried cranberries.

2. *Xuan chi* pickles offset the richness of the rice.

Soak glutinous rice in 4 cups water for 2 hours or overnight. Drain well.

Combine pork and MARINADE ingredients in a bowl in the order listed, mixing well after each addition. Set aside.

To stir-fry, heat 2 tablespoons oil in a wok over medium-high heat. Add pork and stir-fry 1 minute. Add rice, shallots and mushrooms; stir for 1 minute, coating all the rice grains with oil. (Add a little more oil to coat the rice to prevent the grains from sticking together.) Add broth, soy sauce, salt and white pepper to taste. Continue tossing for 4 to 5 minutes until rice is about half cooked and becomes sticky. Add one or two more tablespoons of broth to keep the rice from becoming too sticky or difficult to stir.)

To steam rice in a lotus leaf, submerge leaf for 30 minutes to 1 hour in warm water in a wide roasting pan until soft and pliable. (If there are some holes or tears in a leaf, use two leaves, overlapping the holes so none of the rice leaks through.) Drain leaf (leaves) and discard water. Place leaf in a heat-proof mixing bowl, with edges draped over the rim. Place rice in center of leaf and fold edges of leaf over the rice to enclose completely. Invert a small saucer on top of leaf to hold folds together. Steam for 30 to 45 minutes.

To serve in a lotus leaf, remove bowl from steamer. Remove small saucer. Invert a shallow serving bowl or rimmed platter over the mixing bowl; invert both together and remove mixing bowl. Cut an X-shape or circle around the top of the lotus packet. Lift leaf opening away and garnish top with Chinese parsley and dried shallots. Spoon out rice from packet. Serve with *xuan chi* pickles alongside.

Alternative Steaming Method: Spread rice in a pie dish placed on a steamer rack set over boiling water. Cover steamer and steam for 30 minutes or until rice is done.

To serve, transfer pie dish to table protected with trivet or heat pad. Garnish top of rice with dried shallots and chopped Chinese parsley. Serve with xuan chi pickles alongside.

The key to making Taiwan Aboriginal
Sticky Rice is preparing the sticky
(glutinous) rice so that the grains stay
separated and *al dente.* Wrapping
it in a lotus leaf makes a
dramatic presentation.

Long Life Spinach Noodles

Every Chinese birthday is celebrated by serving noodles such as these because their extra length promises long life and happiness. In this recipe, the juice from the spinach rather than the spinach itself is used for flavoring the noodle dough.

Makes 8 to 10 servings
Cooking time: 15 minutes

⅓ bunch fresh spinach
⅓ cup water

4 cups all-purpose flour
2 eggs, lightly beaten
   Pinch salt

1 cup cornstarch
1 cloth handkerchief (to wrap around cornstarch)

2 quarts water
3 cups cold water
2 tablespoons vegetable oil

Wash spinach thoroughly, cut off and discard stems, and place in a food processor or blender. Add the ⅓ cup water and process until finely chopped. Pour spinach and juice into a bowl through a fine strainer. Further squeeze out excess juice by hand, extracting and saving as much juice as possible. Discard spinach pulp and set juice aside.

Mound flour in a large mixing bowl or on a work surface. Make a deep well in the center and pour in spinach juice, eggs, and salt. Using a chopstick or fork, mix ingredients well and then knead dough into a stiff ball. Cover with a damp cloth and let stand for 10 minutes.

To shape, cut, and cook, follow instructions for making cornstarch bag and for shaping, cutting, and cooking noodles as directed for Fresh Noodles & Wrappers (on page 163).

• Notes •

1. If you have a food processor, you can make the dough in seconds using the metal blade. Process until dough forms a stiff ball.
2. You can also use a manual or electrical pasta machine—it is a lot easier. However, Chinese cooks believe that the warmth of a hand is needed to bring out the best qualities of a dough.
3. Cornstarch is very important in noodle making. Dusting with it gives the dough a smooth feeling without changing the texture. This isn't true when you use additional flour.
4. If you prefer, dry the noodles on a rack and then store in plastic bags for later use.
5. To the Chinese, using the juice from fresh spinach makes much more sense than using the spinach pulp because all the nutrients leach out into the water during processing.
6. Adding cold water, rather than increasing or decreasing the heat, helps maintain a constant cooking temperature. The noodles should be cooked through but still be *al dente* or just tender to the bite like pasta.

Egg Foo Yung

Americans seem to love Egg Foo Yung—perhaps it's because they invented it! That's right, it's not a traditional Chinese dish, but I've included it in my book because it's so popular and because I like it, too. At Chef Chu's we try to vary the recipe to include diced barbecued pork or shrimp or whatever is on hand.

Makes: 4 servings
Cooking time: 20 minutes

MIXTURE

- 4 eggs
- 2 cups bean sprouts, broken into bite-size pieces
- ¼ small white onion, coarsely chopped
- 1 green onion, coarsely chopped
- 2 tablespoons flour
- ¼ teaspoon salt

- ¼ cup vegetable oil

GRAVY

- 2 tablespoons vegetable oil
- 2 tablespoons flour
- 1 cup Rich Chicken Broth (page 52), or chicken bouillon
- 1 tablespoon oyster sauce
- 1 teaspoon dry sherry
- ¼ teaspoon salt
- ¼ teaspoon white pepper

Combine MIXTURE ingredients thoroughly.

To pan-fry, heat wok (or heavy skillet) over moderate heat until hot. Add 2 tablespoons oil and when hot, ladle mixture into 4 mounds in wok. Using a spatula, gently flatten each mound. Cook until underside is brown, turn over, and add remaining 2 tablespoons oil. Continue cooking for 6 to 7 minutes. Remove and drain.

To make gravy, mix oil and flour in a preheated skillet; cook over medium heat to make a roux. Gradually stir in broth along with remaining GRAVY ingredients, cooking until a gravy consistency is reached.

To serve, lightly score top of each patty with an "X" and arrange on serving platter. Spoon sauce over all.

• *Note* •

Try your own variations with this recipe. Add diced pork, chicken, shrimp—whatever—to the gravy.

Peking Meat Sauce Over Noodles

What could be more versatile than an all-purpose tasty meat sauce? Use it just like spaghetti sauce!

Makes: 8 servings
Cooking time: 15 minutes

1 cucumber

8 cups Fresh Noodles (page 162) or purchased noodles

5 dried black mushrooms

2 tablespoons vegetable oil
1 pound ground pork
1 clove garlic, minced or pressed
½ cup shredded bamboo shoots; coarsely chopped
2 pieces pressed bean curd (about 2 inches by 2 inches), diced

SEASONINGS

3 tablespoons soy sauce
1 tablespoon dry sherry
2 tablespoons bean sauce
5 tablespoons Hoisin sauce
¼ teaspoon white pepper
2 cups Rich Chicken Broth (page 52), or chicken bouillon

Cornstarch paste
1 green onion, chopped
1 teaspoon sesame oil

Remove core from cucumber and cut into julienne strips. Refrigerate until ready to use.

Prepare noodles following directions on page 162. Soak mushrooms in warm water for 20 minutes; remove, drain, and mince.

To stir-fry, heat wok (or wide frying pan) over high heat for 1 minute until hot. Add oil and swirl pan to coat sides. When hot, add pork, stirring to separate. Add garlic and cook until fragrant. Add mushrooms, bamboo shoots, bean cake, and SEASONINGS. Cook, stirring occasionally, for about 2 minutes; then thicken with 2 tablespoons cornstarch paste until a spaghetti sauce consistency is reached. Stir in green onion and sesame oil.

Meanwhile, reheat noodles in enough boiling water to cover for about 1 minute; drain and divide into 8 individual serving bowls.

To serve, divide cucumbers and arrange over noodles on one side of each bowl. Spoon sauce over noodles on the other side.

Pan-fried Noodles

Made from simple boiled noodles, Pan-fried Noodles are the authentic Chinese way of preparing Chow Mein.

Makes: 6 servings
Cooking time: 15 minutes

1 recipe Fresh Noodles, page 162
¼ cup vegetable oil

Prepare noodles following directions on page 162.

To pan-fry, heat cast-iron or other heavy-bottom skillet over medium heat. When hot, add oil and swirl pan to coat sides. When oil is hot, add boiled noodles, spreading evenly over bottom of pan. Brown on the bottom without disturbing for 5 to 6 minutes or until golden brown; carefully turn over and brown other side. Remove to a paper towel to drain; serve immediately.

Chow Mein

Chow Mein, in Chinese, simply means fried noodles but I've discovered that in the United States it means something different to everyone. It can be sautéed ingredients in gravy served on top of pan-fried noodles; ingredients and pan-fried noodles that are then sautéed together; or sautéed ingredients served on top of crispy noodles. (The latter is not Chinese, rather, it is an American version.) Here is my version.

Makes: 6 to 8 servings
Cooking time: 15 minutes

2 dried black mushrooms
2 tablespoons vegetable oil
¼ small white onion, cut in slivers
½ cup shredded bamboo shoots
1 stalk celery, thinly sliced on diagonal
1 pound Pan-fried Noodles

SEASONINGS
½ cup chicken broth
2 teaspoons soy sauce
½ teaspoon sugar
½ teaspoon salt
Pinch white pepper

1 cup bean sprouts
1 green onion, split lengthwise and cut into 1-inch pieces
5 snow peas, trimmed and cut in half lengthwise

Soak mushrooms in warm water for 20 minutes; drain, remove stems, and cut into slivers.

To stir-fry, heat wok (or wide frying pan) over high heat for 1 minute until hot. Add oil, swirling pan to coat sides. When oil is hot, add white onion, bamboo shoots, and celery; stir-fry for 30 seconds. Then add noodles, stirring to separate. Stir in SEASONINGS, tossing for 1 minute; adjust taste, if necessary. Add bean sprouts, green onion, mushrooms, and snow peas. Stir-fry for about 1 minute or until bean sprouts are cooked through but not wilted. Serve immediately.

• *Notes* •

1. Barbecued pork strips, cooked shredded chicken, or cooked and peeled shrimp are tasty additions to this dish. Add any cooked meat or seafood along with the bean sprouts.

2. Crispy noodles are egg noodles, deep-fried without ever being boiled. They add crunch but have lost their pasta-like texture.

Pan-fried Angel Hair Noodles *Pictured on page 158*

These Hong Kong-style noodles are fried into a flat pancake—crisp on the outside, soft on the inside—then topped with a deluxe combination of meat, seafood and vegetables and a luscious sauce that permeates the noodles.

Makes: 6 to 8 servings
Cooking time: 15 to 20 minutes

- ½ boneless, skinless chicken breast, sliced
- 12 shrimp, shelled, deveined and patted dry
- 4 or 5 medium sea scallops, thinly sliced crosswise and patted dry
- 6 squid, cleaned, scored, cut into 3 pieces with tentacles and patted dry

MARINADE
- Pinch of salt and white pepper
- 1 egg white
- 1 tablespoon cornstarch

SAUCE
- 2 cups chicken broth
- 3 tablespoons soy sauce
- 1 tablespoon oyster sauce
- 2 teaspoons sugar
- ½ teaspoon salt
- White pepper to taste
- 1 pound Hong Kong-style angel hair noodles

VEGETABLES
- 1 large head broccoli, separated in florets
- 10 snow peas, cut in half diagonally
- 1 small carrot, fancy cut or diagonally sliced
- 12 straw mushrooms
- 12 baby corn, cut in half crosswise
- 3 fresh water chestnuts, sliced into rounds
- ½ cup vegetable oil
- 3 tablespoons vegetable oil
- 2 green onions, cut diagonally into 1-inch slices
- 2 tablespoons cornstarch paste
- 2 teaspoons sesame oil

Place chicken and shrimp in a bowl. Add MARINADE ingredients in the order listed and mix well. Set aside for 15 minutes. Do not marinate the scallops and squid. Combine SAUCE ingredients in another bowl.

To water-blanch, heat 3 quarts water to a boil. Add noodles and blanch for 1 minute until soft, stir to separate. Remove with a strainer and drain. Water-blanch the broccoli, snow peas and carrots for 1 minute. Remove and drain. Set aside with other VEGETABLES.

To pan-fry, heat a 12-inch wide skillet over high heat. Add ½ cup oil and swirl pan to coat bottom and sides. Add noodles, spread and press into an even layer with the bottom of a spatula. Pan-fry over high heat, without disturbing the noodles, until noodles turn evenly golden brown on the bottom, about 5 to 7 minutes. (Noodles should stick together forming a large pancake with a crisp bottom crust.) Using a wide spatula, loosen the noodle pancake and turn over. Pan-fry other side for another 5 to 7 minutes until golden brown and crusty. Lift noodle pancake, letting excess oil drain back into pan; reserve oil for stir-frying. Cut noodles into pie-shaped wedges on a clean cutting board. Arrange noodles in its original round shape on a large rimmed serving platter and keep warm.

To stir-fry, heat a wok over high heat until hot. Add 3 tablespoons reserved oil. Add green onion and stir for 10 seconds until fragrant. Add chicken and shrimp; stir for 30 seconds. Add scallops and squid; stir for 30 seconds. Add VEGETABLES and stir for 30 to 45 seconds. Add SAUCE and bring to a boil. Add cornstarch paste to thicken sauce. Stir in sesame oil. Pour mixture over noodles. There should be enough sauce to generously moisten the noodles.

Simple Boiled Rice

Whether it's boiled, steamed, or even fried, rice is the staple food throughout China. Perhaps the easiest way to prepare it is by boiling. Chinese prefer long-grain rice, simply cooked without even the addition of salt. Traditionally, a heavy-bottomed pot is used to promote an even cooking surface.

Makes: About 7 cups
Cooking time: 30 minutes

3 cups long-grain rice
3 cups water

Wash rice thoroughly by rinsing under cold water.

Combine rice with the 3 cups water in a heavy pot with a tight-fitting lid. Bring to a boil and reduce heat to medium. When water recedes to expose the top of the rice, cover pot and reduce heat to simmer for about 20 minutes. Turn off heat and let stand, without uncovering, for 10 minutes longer. Stir with fork to separate and fluff before serving.

• Note •

Judging the "age" of rice plays a factor in cooking it correctly. New rice softens easily, so use less water; older rice that's tough requires more water. Once you've become accustomed to a certain kind of rice, and have cooked it often enough, you'll be able to tell how "old" your rice is.

Rice Crust

In China, we purposely allow a crust to form on the bottom of the rice pot. After scooping out the boiled rice, we save the crust for deep-frying to be used in soups or other dishes. Or, for a sweet snack, we sprinkle fried rice crust with sugar and eat it like candy.

Makes: 4 servings
Cooking time: 5 minutes

1 recipe Simple Boiled Rice, above

Follow directions for making rice. Remove most of the cooked rice (save for other uses), leaving a thin layer on bottom of pan.

To remove, heat rice pot, uncovered, over low heat until rice becomes dry and crust pulls away from sides of pot. Remove in chunks, let dry completely, and store in plastic bag in a dry place.

Variation: Golden Rice Crust. Follow directions for making rice crust above. Heat 2 cups oil in a wok (or electric deep-fat fryer) to 350°–375°. Carefully, drop chunks of rice into oil and fry for about 45 seconds or until popping and golden brown. Use in soups and other dishes; or sprinkle with sugar for a quick snack.

Congee Rice Porridge   *Pictured on page 161*

What chicken soup is to a Jewish mother, *congee* is to a Chinese cook.

Makes 8 to 10 servings
Cooking time: 30 minutes

1 cup long-grain rice
8 to 10 cups water

Rinse rice thoroughly under running cold water. Drain and place in a large, heavy cast iron or metal pot. Add water and stir.

To cook, bring mixture to a boil, reduce heat to medium, and cook for about 30 minutes or until mixture reaches the consistency of a thick, soup-like porridge.

• *Note* •

You can use leftover cooked rice to make *congee*, too. Reduce the amount of water to 7 or 8 cups but keep the cooking time the same. The result will be a porridge with less starch.

Egg Fried Rice

Egg Fried Rice starts with boiled rice so I use leftover rice that's cold and separates easily. Like so many other basic recipes, you can add just about anything to change the flavor to suit your own taste.

Makes: 8 to 10 servings
Cooking time: 10 minutes

3 tablespoons vegetable oil
2 eggs, lightly beaten
4 cups cold boiled rice

SEASONINGS
2 teaspoons soy sauce
½ teaspoon salt
Pinch white pepper

1 green onion, chopped

To stir-fry, heat wok (or wide frying pan) over high heat. Add 2 tablespoons oil, swirling pan to coat sides. When oil is hot, add eggs and scramble. Remove and set aside. Add remaining 1 tablespoon oil and when hot, add rice. Stir-fry over medium heat for 3 to 4 minutes or until rice separates. Return eggs along with SEASONINGS and toss for about 1 minute until fluffy. Sprinkle with onion, mix well, and serve.

Variation: Pork Fried Rice. Follow directions for making fried rice except: just before stir-frying rice, add ¼ cup diced barbecued pork. After stir-frying rice, mix in 2 tablespoons cooked peas.

Fancy Fried Rice

The more you add the better this rice becomes. We really start with Egg Fried Rice, then stir in shrimp, pork, bean sprouts, peas, roasted peanuts, and a hint of curry powder.

Makes: 8 to 10 servings
Cooking time: 10 minutes

3 tablespoons vegetable oil
2 eggs, slightly beaten
¼ cup diced Chinese Barbecued Pork (page 39 or purchased)
2 tablespoons small cooked shrimp
1 tablespoon chopped white onion
4 cups cold boiled rice

SEASONINGS

2 teaspoons soy sauce
1 teaspoon curry powder (optional)
½ teaspoon salt
Pinch white pepper

1 cup bean sprouts
2 tablespoons cooked peas
2 tablespoons roasted whole peanuts, skins removed

To stir-fry, set wok (or wide frying pan) over high heat. Add 2 tablespoons oil, swirling pan to coat sides. When oil is hot, add eggs and scramble. Remove and set aside. Add remaining oil and when hot, stir in pork, shrimp, and onion. Toss for 1 minute and then add rice. Stir-fry until rice is soft and separates, then add eggs along with SEASONINGS and bean sprouts. Toss to mix well and add peas quickly. Sprinkle with peanuts to serve.

• Notes •

1. Use medium heat to stir-fry rice; later when all ingredients are added, raise the temperature to high to bring out the flavor. Remember to stir constantly to prevent rice from sticking. I always pull the wok off the burner when adding ingredients, then return to heat to stir-fry.

3. You can add a little more oil if the rice begins to stick or a little water if it gets too dry.

4. I first tried serving fried rice with bean sprouts, curry, and peanuts some years ago. My customers always made it a special request so now I offer it to you.

PASTRIES
& DESSERTS

Street vendors aren't common in America, but in China, Hong Kong, and Taiwan they sell a huge variety of snacks from early morning till late at night. These snacks, such as steamed buns or dumplings, are called *dim sum*—which loosely translated means "close to the heart" or "to please the heart." *Dim sum* pastries are served as breakfast nibbles as people hurry off to work and then late in the evening as a pick-me-up after a shift of work or as one strolls the streets and parks or socializes with friends. *Dim sum* pastries have become very popular in America as well, although they are served in restaurants rather than from street vendors.

The savory pastry recipes that follow are wonderful as luncheon treats or teatime morsels. We've included only the most celebrated of the hundreds of varieties of *dim sum* featured on our menus over the years. The most popular, the Potsticker, is so named because when properly made, it sticks to the pot! The dumpling is first steamed gently in a frying pan with a little

water, then when the water evaporates, it is pan-fried until crusty brown on the bottom and becomes slightly stuck to the pan, so the juices are sealed in until you take the first luscious bite. Baked Sesame Buns are a savory new offering we serve alone as a snack or filled with Silk Road Lamb as an entree. And as is the case with most *dim sum*, if there are any leftovers, you can store them in the refrigerator and reheat in a steamer, microwave or oven—they will disappear quickly.

Chinese desserts are artful and tasty but sometimes don't satisfy the American craving for a rich, sweet finale to a meal because Chinese, as a rule, do not have a "sweet tooth." Our desserts are lightly sweetened and subtly flavored. I urge you to try the recipes that follow! Almond Cream Squares are light and spongy and have the texture of jello or rich custard. Eight Treasure Rice Pudding is an impressive traditional-style fruit-studded pudding served after a traditional dinner. Two of our newest and most delectable desserts, Pineapple Crescents and Sesame Taro Rolls, are ones we serve at the end of special banquets. Or, you may decide to forego a fancy dessert and follow the common Chinese custom of bringing out a basket of fresh fruit!

Chinese pastries are eaten at meals and as snacks, and include both savory and sweet varieties. Pineapple Crescents (page 188) is a fresh take on dessert raviolis.

Basic Bread Dough

What a rich chicken broth is to a soup, this basic bread dough is to many of my Chinese pastries or snacks. You're lost without it! Even in China, a cook's all-purpose steamed bread dough is the basis for any type of dumpling, cake, or bun.

Makes: 1 recipe dough
Cooking time: None

- ¾ cup warm water (about 110°F)
- 1 tablespoon sugar
- ½ cup warm milk (about 110°F)
- ½ package active dry yeast
- 4 cups all-purpose flour
- ½ teaspoon baking powder

Combine water and sugar well. Stir in milk and check temperature (it should be about 110°F). Add yeast, stirring to dissolve, and set aside until mixture begins to bubble. Gradually add flour, mixing as you go. Knead for 3 to 4 minutes and shape into a ball and cover with a damp cloth to rise in a warm, draft-free spot for about 1 hour or until doubled in size.

Turn dough out onto a floured board, flatten slightly, and sprinkle surface with baking powder. Knead for about 5 minutes until smooth. Set aside, covered, until ready to use.

Butterfly Steamed Bread

The name gives away the festive shape of these simple buns. I usually serve them as an accompaniment to all types of duck, Five-spice Beef, or Chinese Barbecued Pork.

Makes: 24 snacks
Cooking time: 15 minutes

- 1 recipe Basic Bread Dough (above)
- 2 tablespoons vegetable oil
   Decorative stamp and red food coloring

Prepare dough as directed above.

To shape, roll dough into a cylinder about 1-inch in diameter. Cut cylinder into pieces 1½-inch wide. With cut side up, press dough down with palm to flatten. Brush upper edge of pancake with oil; fold pancake in half (oil side in) and press down lightly to seal. With thumb and index finger, pinch together along folded edge to seal tightly. Using a thick utensil such as a cleaver, make 3 indentations along curved edge. Place on a floured cookie sheet to rise in a warm place for 10 minutes.

To steam, line the inside of a bamboo steamer with wet cheesecloth to prevent sticking. Arrange buns on cheesecloth, cover, and steam over boiling water for about 12 minutes.

To decorate, remove buns and let cool slightly. Dip stamp into red food coloring and then onto surface of bun.

Baked Sesame Buns

These small flaky buns, filled with a savory scallion-bacon filling, are often called "crab buns" because their puffy shapes resemble freshwater crabs.

Makes: 24 to 26 buns
Cooking time: 20 minutes

WATER DOUGH

- 3 cups all-purpose flour
- 1 cup cold water
- 2 eggs, beaten
- ¼ stick butter (2 tablespoons) or substitute butter spread (cut in pieces)

OIL DOUGH

- 3 cups all-purpose flour
- 1¾ sticks butter (14 tablespoons) or substitute butter spread (cut in ½-inch pieces)

FILLING

- 1 pound lean bacon, diced ½-inch, separate the pieces
- 1 cup thinly sliced green onions
- 1 egg white
- 1 cup sesame seeds

• *Notes* •

1. Vegetarian Alternative: omit the bacon and increase the green onions. You may also add minced carrot, mushrooms or Chinese yellow chives to the filling.

2. Store in an airtight plastic bag in the refrigerator.

To make WATER DOUGH, mix ingredients together in a bowl. Knead dough on a lightly floured board until smooth and elastic. Return dough to bowl, cover with a damp cloth and let rest while you prepare OIL DOUGH.

To make OIL DOUGH, knead butter into the flour on a lightly floured board until smooth and elastic. Gather dough into a ball and set aside for 10 minutes.

To make FILLING, mix FILLING ingredients together in a bowl.

To assemble dough, on a lightly floured board, roll out WATER DOUGH into a large 16-inch circle. Place OIL DOUGH in the center of WATER DOUGH. Pull up edges of WATER DOUGH around the OIL DOUGH to encase it completely. Pinch edges of WATER DOUGH to seal. Place pinched seam side down on the board. Roll dough ball into a 15x15-inch rectangle. Fold the dough in half, matching edges; fold in half again to make 4 layers. Turn the dough a quarter turn, and repeat rolling and folding procedure 4 more times to make many layers.

Roll the dough into a ⅛-inch thick rectangle about 24x18 inches wide. Cut the rectangle in half lengthwise, making two 24x9-inch rectangles. From the long side, roll each piece of dough tightly into a long cylinder 24 inches long by about 1 inch in diameter. Cut off uneven ends. Slice each cylinder crosswise into 12 equal pieces, making 24 total. Keep pieces covered with a bowl while you assemble buns.

To assemble buns, place a piece of dough with the spiral surfaces visible on the sides. With a rolling pin, flatten the dough into a 3-inch circle, making the edges a little thinner than the middle. Place a rounded teaspoon of FILLING in the center. Pull up edges; pinch together to seal. With seam side down, pat each bun into a ⅓-inch thick round. Set buns apart on a tray. Brush tops of buns with egg white and dredge in sesame seeds placed in a dish. Place seed-side up, slightly apart, on a lightly greased cooking sheet or pizza stone.

To bake, preheat oven to 425°. Place cooking sheet on an oven rack set 8 inches from the broiler. Bake buns for 24 minutes until light-colored and puffy. Turn on the broiler to 500°. Broil buns for another 2 to 3 minutes until tops turn golden brown. Watch carefully to prevent burning. Transfer buns to a rack; cool slightly. Serve buns hot or warm.

Steamed Pork Buns

Prepared bread dough is shaped into buns and then filled with a stuffing made of diced barbecued pork, green onion, and flavorful oyster sauce. When steamed, they become puffy and white. Pork buns are prepared all over China though they originated in Canton province.

Makes: 12 to 18 snacks
Cooking time: 25 minutes

- 1 recipe Basic Bread Dough (page 176)
- 1 tablespoon vegetable oil

FILLING
- ½ pound Chinese Barbecued Pork (page 39), diced
- 1 green onion (white part), minced
- ½ cup chicken broth
- 3 tablespoons oyster sauce
- 1 tablespoon dry sherry
- 1 tablespoon sugar
- ¼ teaspoon salt

  Cornstarch paste
- ½ teaspoon sesame oil

Prepare dough as directed on page 176.

To stir-fry, heat wok (or wide frying pan) over high heat for 1 minute until hot. Add oil and swirl pan to coat sides. When oil is hot, add pork and onion, stirring for 30 seconds. Mix in broth, oyster sauce, sherry, sugar, and salt. Bring to a boil, thicken with 1 tablespoon cornstarch paste, and sprinkle with sesame oil. Transfer to a bowl, cool, and refrigerate until thickened.

To assemble, roll dough into a cylinder about 2 inches in diameter. Cut cylinder into pieces 1½ inches wide. With a cut side up, press down with palm of hand to flatten. Place 1 table-spoon filling in center of dough. Gather up edges of dough around filling in loose folds. Bring folds together at top and twist securely to make a stem as illustrated. Let rise in a warm place for 10 minutes.

To steam, line the inside of a bamboo steamer with wet cheesecloth. Arrange buns on cheesecloth, cover, and steam over boiling water for 12 minutes.

1) Place 1 tablespoon filling in center of flattened dough. Gather up edges around filling in loose folds. Bring together at top and 2) twist securely to seal and make a small stem.

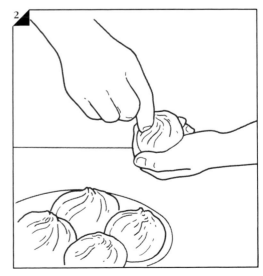

Shanghai Pan-fried Dumplings

Really a first cousin to Chinese potstickers, this dumpling differs slightly in the texture after cooking. The top is soft while the bottom is chewy and crunchy. Traditionally, pan-fried dumplings are eaten at breakfast or as a snack rather than during a meal.

Makes: 24 snacks
Cooking time: 15 minutes

1 recipe Basic Bread Dough (page 176)

FILLING
- ½ pound ground pork
- 1 head bok choy, cored and coarsely chopped
- 1 green onion, minced
- 2 thumb-size slices fresh ginger, minced
- 2 water chestnuts, chopped
- 1 teaspoon sesame oil
- ½ teaspoon sugar
- 1 teaspoon salt

- Black sesame seeds or sesame seeds
- 3 tablespoons vegetable oil
- ½ cup water

Prepare dough as directed on page 176.

Combine FILLING ingredients well and refrigerate until firm.

To assemble, roll dough into a cylinder about 1 inch in diameter. Cut cylinder into 24 pieces, each about 1½ inches wide. With cut side up, flatten pieces with palm of hand. Fill each center with 1 tablespoon filling. Pull edges of dough up over filling, twisting a small stem where drawn together as illustrated. Sprinkle tops with sesame seeds.

To pan-fry, heat a cast-iron or other heavy-bottom skillet over moderate heat. Add oil, swirling to coat bottom. Put buns in skillet, pour in water, and cover with a tight-fitting lid. Cook for about 8 minutes without removing cover. When water has evaporated, remove lid and let buns brown slightly for 2 to 3 minutes (watch carefully to prevent burning).

1) Spread 1 tablespoon filling in center of flattened dough. 2) Pull edges of dough up over filling. 3) pleating as you go, and 4) twist securely at top to seal and make a small stem.

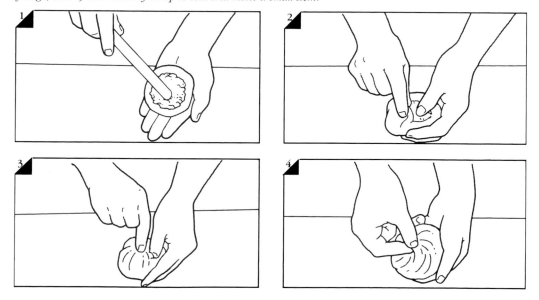

Sesame Taro Rolls *Pictured on facing page and 214*

Everyone loves these! Their slightly sweet, mild coconut flavor is accented with the light crunch of sesame seeds.

Makes: 10 servings
Cooking time: 8 to 10 minutes

½ loaf good-quality, unsliced fine-textured white bread, frozen

FILLING

1½ pounds of taro root, peeled and cut in chunks (see Note)
½ cup vegetable oil
¾ cup sugar
1 tablespoon coconut cream

SEALING PASTE

¼ cup water
¼ cup flour

1 egg, beaten
¼ cup sesame seeds

1 quart vegetable oil (fresh, not previously used)

Powdered confectioners sugar
Mint sprigs

To serve, place 2 rolls on each individual serving plate. Dust lightly with powdered sugar. Garnish with a mint sprig. Or, these rolls may be served with ice cream, fresh berries or sliced fruit.

• Note •

You may substitute the same amount of fresh peeled yams for the taro. Cook and use as directed for the taro root. Add a little grated orange rind to the taro or yam filling to give it a different flavor.

To prepare bread, slice the frozen loaf crosswise into thin ⅛-inch thick slices using a sharp serrated knife or cleaver. Make 20 slices. Stack four slices evenly together and trim off the crusts, making the slices about 4 inches-square. Trim remaining slices. Using a rolling pin, flatten each slice to compress it making it easier to roll during assembly and to produce a delicate thin crust on the outside of the rolls. Cover slices with a slightly damp towel to prevent drying.

To make FILLING, place taro pieces in a pie dish set on a steamer rack. Cover and steam over boiling water for 20 minutes until very soft. Drain well. Purée taro in a food processor. Heat ¼ cup oil in a wok over medium heat. Add taro. Stir constantly until it comes to a boil. Add sugar and coconut cream while stirring. Reduce heat and add remaining ¼ cup oil. Continue stirring 12 to 15 minutes until taro mixture becomes thick, glossy and translucent. It should hold together in a mass. Lower heat and stir constantly to prevent burning. To test for doneness, cool mixture slightly and press it with your finger. It should leave an indentation and not stick to your finger. Transfer to a shallow bowl to cool.

To assemble, mix SEALING PASTE ingredients in a small bowl. Place egg and sesame seeds in separate shallow dishes. Lay a bread slice on a work surface. Roll a heaping tablespoon of FILLING with your hands into a ½-inch diameter cylinder about 4-inches long to match the width of the slice. Place FILLING along the nearest edge of the slice; dab some SEALING PASTE along the farthest edge. Roll the bread slice to enclose the filling, pressing edges together to seal. Gently cut each roll in half crosswise to make two 2-inch rolls. Place rolls apart on a tray. (This can be done up to a week ahead. Freeze rolls apart on trays, then place in an airtight plastic bag. Thaw completely before continuing.) Dip cut ends into beaten egg; dredge in sesame seeds. Set apart on a tray.

To deep-fry, heat 1 quart of oil in a wok to 300°. Gently lower 8 to 10 rolls into oil and fry for about 2 minutes until lightly golden. Drain well. Fry remaining rolls in batches.

To deep-fry again, reheat oil in wok to 365°. Fry all the rolls at once in oil for 10 to 15 seconds until light golden tan (do not brown) and the wrapper becomes crisp. Remove and drain.

Sesame Taro Rolls are a delicious
mix of tastes and textures: smooth
taro filling , rich coconut cream,
finished off with a sesame seed
crunch. It's a real show-
stopping dessert!

Steamed Silver Thread Buns

Because rice is rarely served at a banquet, Chinese often present dumplings or other pastries such as these fancy-shaped ones. Originating from Hunan, they have been adapted to be served as a snack as well.

Makes: 12 snacks
Cooking time: 20 minutes

1 recipe Basic Bread Dough (page 176)
5 tablespoons lard (or vegetable shortening)
¼ teaspoon salt
2 tablespoons sugar
2 tablespoons minced Virginia ham or other ham

Prepare dough as directed on page 176.

To shape, flatten dough slightly and put in 2 tablespoons lard and salt. Knead well for 5 minutes. Roll out into a rectangle about ¼-inch thick. Spread with remaining 3 tablespoons lard and sprinkle with sugar. Fold dough into thirds, like a letter, to make a rectangle.

Cut off 5 thin slivers from end of rectangle for each bun. Holding tops of slivers together, gently stretch dough until it reaches 6 inches long. Starting at one end and still holding slices together, roll dough into a ball. Tuck end into opening at top (or bottom) to secure as illustrated.

Sprinkle tops with just a little ham and let stand for about 10 minutes.

To steam, line the inside of a steamer with a wet towel to prevent sticking. Arrange buns in steamer, cover, and steam over boiling water for about 10 minutes.

1) Cut off 5 thin slivers of dough from end, making a piece. (Cut remaining dough in same way, making a total of 12 pieces.) Rotate piece of dough a quarter-turn, and 2) holding ends of slivers together, gently stretch until dough reaches 6 inches long. 3) Starting at one end, wrap dough round and round in a spiral shape and then 4) tuck end into opening at top to secure.

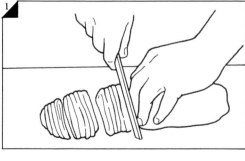

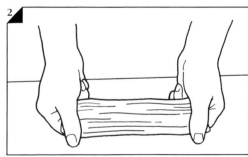

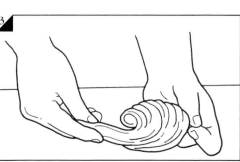

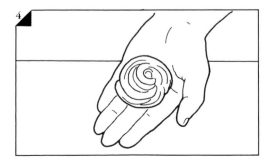

Four-season Dumplings

Your guests will think you spent hours making these colorful gourmet snacks. After shaping bread dough around a spoonful of seasoned meat filling, you top the cloverleaf dumpling with four seasons' toppings: finely minced white onion, carrot, black mushroom, and Chinese parsley.

Makes: 24 snacks
Cooking time: 15 minutes

- 2 cups all-purpose flour
- ¼ cup boiling water
- ¼ cup cold water

FOUR SEASONS TOPPINGS
- 3 dried black mushrooms
- ¼ small white onion, minced
- 2 teaspoons minced carrot
- 10 stalks Chinese parsley (cilantro), minced

FILLING
- ½ pound ground pork
- 10 medium-size prawns, minced (optional)
- ¼ teaspoon minced fresh ginger
- 1 green onion (white part), minced
- 2 tablespoons bamboo shoots, minced
- ¾ teaspoon salt
  Pinch white pepper
- ¼ teaspoon sugar
- ¼ teaspoon sesame oil

  Bok choy or lettuce leaves

  Hot Chili Oil (page 212), or purchased
  Red rice vinegar
  Soy sauce

To make dough, combine flour and boiling water together in a mixing bowl, then stir in cold water. Shape into a ball and then turn out onto a floured board; knead for about 3 minutes. Cover with a damp towel and set aside for 10 minutes.

Meanwhile, soak mushrooms in warm water for 20 minutes; drain, remove stems, and mince. Set aside with remaining FOUR SEASONS TOPPINGS.

Combine FILLING ingredients thoroughly; refrigerate.

To assemble, knead dough again for 3 to 5 minutes until smooth. Roll into a cylinder 1-inch in diameter. Cut off ends, then cut into pieces ¾-inch wide. With a cut side up, press dough down with palm to flatten. Roll out with rolling pin into pancakes 2½-inches wide.

Place 1 teaspoon filling in center of pancake. Join opposite sides of pancake together by pinching at the top; then pinch remaining (opposite) sides at top to form a square with 4 holes—it should look like a 4-leaf clover. With a finger, spread open each hole slightly, pushing filling down to the bottom. Place dumplings on a cookie sheet and partially freeze.

To decorate, drop some white onion into the first hole, carrot in the second, black mushrooms in the third, and parsley into the fourth. Repeat for remaining dumplings.

To steam, line the inside of a steamer with bok choy leaves. Arrange dumplings in steamer, cover, and steam over boiling water for about 10 minutes.

To serve, without removing cover, bring steamer to the table on a large serving platter. Lift off lid to serve with dipping sauce made of chili oil, vinegar, and soy sauce in proportions to suit your taste.

• Notes •

1. You can chop the filling ingredients together in a food processor—just don't overprocess so that the ingredients lose their texture.

2. Partially freezing the dumplings before decorating helps to retain the shape and firmness.

Lichee Nut Blossoms

Lichee nuts come from the tropical regions of China and are used often when preparing simple Chinese desserts such as this one. A number of other fruits may be substituted or added depending on the season. We added kumquats, watermelon, and kiwi for the dessert pictured below.

Makes: 4 servings
Cooking time: None

- 4 champagne or other stemmed glasses
  Crushed ice
- 1 can (10 oz.) seedless lichee nuts, drained
- 4 maraschino cherries
- 1 ounce Cointreau

Fill each champagne glass half full of crushed ice. Distribute lichee nuts equally among glasses. Top each dessert with a cherry and a splash of Cointreau.

Variation: Rainbow Fruit Cups. Layer kumquats, loquats, and lichee nuts in regular or tall parfait glasses to create a rainbow effect. Use fewer kumquats since they are stronger in flavor than loquats and lichee nuts. Top with cherries and Cointreau as directed above, or with slices of kiwi.

• *Note* •
You can substitute Triple Sec or other fruity liquers for Cointreau if desired.

Potstickers

Here's a typical Northern Chinese pastry that's well-known and prepared throughout the world. Though eaten as a snack in China, I find that most Americans serve potstickers as an appetizer.

Makes: About 2 dozen
Cooking time: 15 minutes

DOUGH
2 cups all-purpose flour
½ cup water

FILLING
½ pound ground pork
½ small head Chinese (Napa) cabbage, cored and chopped
1 green onion, coarsely chopped
2 thumb-size slices fresh ginger, minced
2 water chestnuts, chopped
1 teaspoon salt
½ teaspoon sugar
   Pinch white pepper
1 teaspoon sesame oil

5 tablespoons vegetable oil
1 cup water

   Hot chili oil
   Red rice vinegar
   Soy Sauce

In a bowl, combine flour and water, mixing to form a ball. Remove to a floured board and knead with palm of hand for about 3 minutes. Shape into a ball, cover with damp towel, and let stand for about 10 minutes.

To make filling, combine FILLING ingredients well and refrigerate until ready to use.

To shape and assemble, knead dough for about 3 minutes. Roll into a cylinder that is about 1 inch in diameter. Cut off ends, then cut into about 24 pieces, each ¾-inch wide. With a cut side up, press dough down with palm to flatten. Roll out with a rolling pin to make pancakes about 2½ inches in diameter.

Spoon 1 tablespoon filling into center of each pancake. Fold dough over to make half circle and pleat edges firmly together.

To pan-fry, heat cast-iron or other heavy-bottom skillet over moderate heat. Add 3 tablespoons oil swirling to coat bottom. When oil is hot, place potstickers, seam side up, in skillet and agitate (shake) for 30 seconds. Pour in water, cover, and gently boil over moderate heat for 7 to 8 minutes. When oil and water start to sizzle, add remaining 2 tablespoons oil. Tip skillet to distribute oil evenly; watch carefully (uncovered)) to prevent sticking. When bottoms are brown, remove from heat and carefully lift out potstickers with spatula.

To serve, turn potstickers over (dark side up) and arrange on serving platter. Combine chili oil, vinegar, and soy sauce in proportions to suit your taste and offer sauce for dipping.

• Notes •

1. You can freeze uncooked potstickers for later use but remember to squeeze out the water from cabbage during preparation (in a colander or cheesecloth). Freeze potstickers separately on cookie sheets until firm, then put them in plastic bags.

2. When rolling out the pancakes, leave the centers slightly thicker than the edges. A thicker center will hold up better during the browning.

3. If you prefer, steam potstickers for about 12 minutes over boiling water instead of pan-frying.

Follow the many complex flavors of a Chinese meal with a simple, chilled dessert of sliced kiwi, kimquats, watermelon, and lichee nuts, offered in glass stemware filled with shaved ice and Cointreau. (Recipe on page 184.)

185

Shanghai Onion Cakes

Cooked within the several layers of dough are concealed, aromatic green onions. A delicious snack.

Makes: 24 snacks
Cooking time: 25 minutes

- 2 cups all-purpose flour
- ½ cup boiling water
- ¼ cup cold water

  Vegetable oil
- 1 teaspoon salt
- 2 green onions,
  coarsely chopped

- 2 tablespoons lard,
  vegetable oil, or chopped
  bacon

To shape, mix flour and boiling water with chopsticks in a bowl; then add cold water. Remove to a board and knead with palm of hand for 3 minutes. Cover with a damp towel for 10 minutes. Then knead again for 3 to 5 minutes. Roll into a cylinder about 2 inches in diameter. Cut cylinder into 6 sections.

With either cut side up, press dough down with palm to flatten. Roll out into 7- or 8-inch pancakes.

To assemble, brush each surface of pancake with oil. Sprinkle evenly with a pinch of salt and chopped green onion. Roll up jellyroll fashion; then wind jellyroll in a spiral (it should look like a snail). Flatten slightly with heel of palm; then flatten more with rolling pin, making each "snail" about 5 inches in diameter.

To pan-fry, heat a cast-iron or other heavy-bottom skillet over moderate heat. Brush with oil. When hot, fry pancake on both sides for about 5 to 6 minutes total or until it turns brown and a crust is formed. Remove and wrap in a dry towel to keep warm. Cut into fourths to serve.

Mandarin Pancakes   *Pictured on page 116*

Simple-to-make pancakes that serve as "wrappers" for Peking Duck or Mu Shu Pork.

Makes: 1½ dozen
Cooking time: 40 minutes

  2 cups all-purpose flour
  ½ cup boiling water
  ¼ cup cold water

     Vegetable oil

To shape, mix flour and boiling water with chopsticks in a bowl; then add cold water. Remove to a board and knead with palm of hand for 3 minutes. Cover with a damp towel for 10 minutes. Then knead again for 3 to 5 minutes. Roll into a cylinder about 1½-inches in diameter. Cut off ends, then cut cylinder into 1½-inch-thick pieces.

With either cut side up, press dough down with palm to flatten. Brush one pancake with oil, then place another pancake on top. Roll out into a 5- or 6-inch pancake.

To pan-fry, heat cast-iron or other heavy-bottom skillet over moderate heat. Brush with oil. When hot, cook pancake on both sides for about 1 minute on each side or until it starts to puff and turn lightly brown. Remove from pan, separating into 2 pancakes (they come apart easily). Wrap in dry towel to retain moisture.

To serve, reheat pancakes, wrapped in a damp towel, in steamer for about 5 minutes; keep warm.

Pineapple Crescents *Pictured on page 174, 215*

This is my version of a dessert ravioli I enjoyed in Southeast Asia. I use fresh pineapple instead of pasta to enfold the filling, then serve it with a light and heavenly sauce.

Makes: 24 crescents to serve 12 (allow 2 per person)
Cooking time: (including prep time) 1 hour

SAUCE

- 1 cup water
- 3 thumb-size slices of ginger
- 1 (6 ounce) can pineapple juice
- 1 tablespoon sugar
- 2 teaspoons lemon juice (to taste)

- 2 teaspoons cornstarch paste

FILLING

- 8 ounces mascarpone cheese
- 16 to 20 canned seeded lichees, drained and quartered
- 4 slices candied ginger, minced

- 1 whole pineapple, ends trimmed and peeled into a round cylinder

GARNISH

- 3 tablespoons chopped Hunan Candied Pecans (page 43)
- 8 fresh mint leaf tips
  Fresh fruit: strawberries, raspberries, blueberries, sliced figs or kiwi

To simmer SAUCE, bring water and ginger to a boil in a medium saucepan. Boil for 2 minutes. Add remaining SAUCE ingredients and return a boil. Thicken with cornstarch paste. Remove from heat. Strain SAUCE, discard ginger and chill. The SAUCE should be slightly sweet and tart. (This can be made up to 1 day ahead, covered and refrigerated.)

Combine FILLING ingredients in a bowl and mix well. Set aside. (This can be done ahead and chilled.)

Slice pineapple into rounds about ⅛-inch thick. Set slices aside on a plastic wrap-lined tray. Make 24 to 26 slices (you might make a few extra in case a few break).

To water-blanch, bring 2 cups water to a boil in a saucepan. Poach a few pineapple slices at a time for about 30 to 45 seconds until the slice becomes flexible enough to fold in half. Lift slices out with a flat strainer to prevent breaking. Place slices on a surface in a single layer until cool enough to handle.

To assemble, place 1 teaspoon of FILLING mixture on the center of pineapple. (See Note.) Fold pineapple in half to enclose filling to make a crescent shape. Press around edges to eliminate air. Place crescents on a plastic-wrap lined tray in a single layer. Cover crescents with plastic wrap and store in the refrigerator until serving time. (The SAUCE and crescents can be made up to a day ahead and kept chilled until ready to serve.)

Chill serving plates ready for serving.

To serve, place 2 pineapple crescents on a chilled plate, spoon the pineapple sauce over top, garnish with chopped Candied Pecans and a mint leaf tip. Garnish with fresh berries or sliced fruit. We also like to serve this dessert with ice cream or sorbet.

• Notes •

1. To help in folding the pineapple slices, use a square of plastic wrap. Fill a pineapple slice on top of the wrap. Pull up the pineapple slice using the plastic wrap to help fold it in half and give the pineapple support to prevent breaking.

2. You may substitute jackfruit for the lichee in the filling.

Banana Sesame

A typical Chinese dinner concludes with fresh fruit. Banana Sesame—bite-size pieces of fried banana sweetened with toasted sesame seeds and powdered sugar—is a tropical adaptation popular in Taiwan and South China.

Makes: 6 servings
Cooking time: 15 minutes

BATTER

- ¾ cup flour
- ½ cup cornstarch
- ½ teaspoon baking powder
  Pinch salt
  Pinch sugar
- ¾ cup water
- 1 teaspoon vegetable oil
  Few drops yellow food coloring (optional)

- 2 firm ripe bananas

  Vegetable oil, for deep-frying

- 2 tablespoons sesame seeds, lightly toasted
- 2 tablespoons powdered sugar

Combine BATTER ingredients using a wire whisk; let stand for 30 minutes.

Peel bananas and slice diagonally into pieces, dropping into batter; set aside.

To deep-fry, heat 4 cups oil in a wok (or electric deep-fat fryer) to 300°. Using a toothpick, pick up coated banana and let drain; carefully drop into oil and deep-fry for about 2 minutes or until a crust is formed. Remove, drain on paper towels, and trim off uneven parts of crust. Remove any batter particles in oil.

To deep-fry again, raise oil temperature to 350°. Return bananas and fry for about 2 minutes or until golden brown. Remove, drain on paper towels, and arrange on serving platter.

To serve, crush sesame seeds with rolling pin and combine with sugar. Sprinkle on bananas to serve.

• *Note* •

You can eliminate the sesame seed/sugar mixture and simply arrange fried bananas on a bed of fresh sweetened whipped cream.

Almond Cream Squares

I'd describe this refreshing almond-flavored dessert as a cross between jello, custard, and sponge cake. It tastes best when served cold.

Makes: 8 to 10 servings
Cooking time: 5 minutes

2 quarts water
1 ounce agar-agar
½ cup sugar
1½ cups milk
¾ to 1 ounce almond extract

Fruit cocktail or other fresh fruit in light syrup

Bring water to a boil in saucepan. Stir in agar-agar until completely dissolved. Add sugar and stir until dissolved. Remove from heat and add milk and almond extract. Pour into a shallow pan and chill until firm.

To serve, cut chilled mixture into ½-inch cubes; spoon into serving dishes and top with fruit.

• *Notes* •

1. Change the flavor to coconut by eliminating the almond extract and substituting coconut milk for regular milk. Add 1 ounce flaked coconut before chilling as well.

2. For a more dramatic presentation, chill almond mixture in a 2- to 2½-quart mold. To serve, invert mold onto platter and arrange fruit around base.

Eight-Treasure Rice Pudding *Pictured on facing page*

Probably the most impressive dessert in terms of presentation, this sweet dish resembles a jewel-studded crown and is served traditionally at banquets or on holidays.

Makes: 10 to 12 servings
Cooking time: 1½ hours

2 cups sweet rice
   (glutinous rice)

FRUITS
10 preserved dragon eyes
    (or any preserved fruit)
6 preserved red dates
2 tablespoons raisins
2 pieces preserved candied
   kumquat, chopped
12 candied lotus seeds
1 maraschino cherry, halved
3 preserved green plums,
   cut in fourths

¼ cup vegetable oil
½ cup sugar
½ can (10 oz.) red bean
   paste

SYRUP
¼ cup sugar
1 cup cold water

   Cornstarch paste

Soak rice in warm water for 2 hours or overnight; drain well.

To steam, line the inside of a steamer with wet cheesecloth. Place rice on cheesecloth, cover, and steam over boiling water for 25 minutes.

Meanwhile, soak dragon eyes in warm water for 10 minutes; drain and cut into small pieces. Also soak dates in warm water for 10 minutes; drain and cut into fourths.

To assemble, line 2 small bowls (about 1 quart each) that are suitable for steaming with plastic wrap. Combine rice, oil, and sugar together. Evenly divide half the rice (reserving other half) between both bowls; press rice up the sides of bowl to line, forming a well in the center.

Mix reserved half of rice with raisins, kumquats, dragon eyes, and some of the lotus seeds. Spoon all but 1 cup rice mixture into each well, still keeping a small well in the center. Fill each small well with half the bean paste, then cover entirely with remaining rice mixture.

Invert bowls on a plate and carefully remove (plastic lining should remain in bowls). Arrange plums, dates, cherries, and remaining lotus seeds decoratively on mounds as illustrated. Carefully put plastic-lined bowls back onto rice mounds and turn right side up.

To steam again, place bowls on rack in steamer, cover, and steam over boiling water for about 1 hour.

Meanwhile, combine SYRUP ingredients in a saucepan. Bring to a boil and then thicken with 1 tablespoon cornstarch paste until the consistency of syrup is reached.

To serve, invert bowls on serving plate and remove plastic wrap. Pour syrup over mounds.

• *Notes* •

1. Plastic wrap is essential—it keeps the rice mixture from sticking to the bowls.

2. The rice should be very soft; the longer you steam it, the more flavorful it becomes.

3. The "eight treasures" can be varied according to your taste. Choose any preserved candy or fruit.

191

TIPS & TECHNIQUES

Good cutting technique requires skill. I have learned that it takes years of practice to acquire proficiency. An old saying in China says this well: knowledgeable people can tell how accomplished the chef is by the appearance of his cuts. The real art of cutting is to make cuts perfectly even.

How important is cutting correctly? First, it contributes to the aesthetics of an attractive dish. Secondly, it affects the overall cooking time of the ingredients. Many Chinese recipes that specify a short cooking time rely on ingredients that are uniformly cut and are the same size, to insure that they will cook evenly.

You may not become proficient at cutting right away. However, the information in this section and the illustrations on page 194 should help you to understand just what to strive for. Keep in mind that practice does make perfect, and you'll master these skills naturally as you cook.

Here's a short description of cutting techniques used in Chinese cooking:

Slicing: to cut into thin pieces, $1/16$- to $1/8$-inch thick and 1 to $1^1/2$ inches across

Slant-cutting: to slice diagonally, usually $1/4$- to $1/2$-inch thick

Dicing: to cut into $1/2$-inch cubes

Cubing: to cut into $3/4$-inch cubes

Roll-cutting: to cut into uniform triangular-shaped pieces

Shredding or Julienne: to slice finely into matchstick-size pieces

Shaving: to cut into paper-thin slices

Chopping: to cut into pieces

Smashing or Crushing: to flatten ingredient, using the side of a cleaver or large knife

Processing: to cut using different blades of a food processor

Great chefs—and good cooks!—work to perfect their cutting techniques so that ingredients are uniform in size and cooking time.

Cutting Techniques

1) Slicing and 2) dicing are the most common cutting methods. 3) Roll-cutting into triangular pieces is accomplished by rotating vegetable $1/3$ turn each time cut is made. 4) Shredding and 5) smashing (flattening) are other ways to prepare Chinese ingredients.

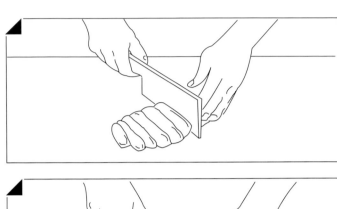

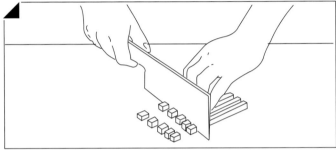

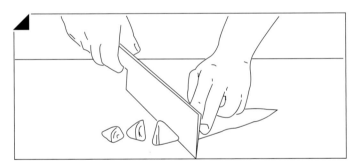

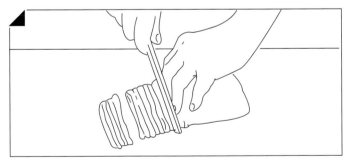

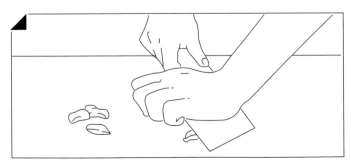

Slicing

The shape of the slice depends on what ingredient you're cutting, but a good rule of thumb to remember is "no piece should be larger than bite-size nor thicker than $1/2$-inch."

When slicing meat, cut against the grain to expose more surface. Slices are usually about $1/4$- x $1/2$- x $1/2$-inch in size. To make slicing easier, partially freeze meat or poultry just before cutting.

Fish should be sliced with the grain; you may have to cut the fish into sections first if it is too large to slice as is.

Slant-cutting

Slice firm vegetables such as celery, bok choy and asparagus on the diagonal to expose more of the surface and reduce cooking time. Slant-cutting some meats such as flank steak also aids in tenderizing because it breaks down tissues or texture.

Dicing & Cubing

Any ingredient that has been cut into a small piece could be called a dice, a cube, or a chunk. The difference between them is size.

Dicing usually produces a piece no larger than $1/2$-inch square, while a cube can measure up to $3/4$-inch square. A chunk is larger still—up to 1-inch in diameter.

When cutting an ingredient with unstable sides or an uneven size, such as ginger root, cut a thin slice off the top, turn it over, cut-side down to stabilize it, and then continue cutting.

Roll-cutting

Cutting a cylindrical vegetable such as a carrot or turnip so that it cooks evenly is tricky. Roll-cutting—slicing into triangular pieces—is accomplished while rotating the vegetable. Once the pieces are cut, two sides or surfaces are exposed, thus creating a greater area for absorbing seasoning during cooking.

Make a diagonal cut near one end of the vegetable, rotate it $1/3$ of a turn and make a second diagonal cut so that the new cut meets the first one. You've now created a new surface. Continue to roll and cut until you reach the end of the vegetable.

Shredding or Julienne

Shredding or julienne is really just slicing, and then slicing again perpendicular to the slices, to produce thread-like matchstick pieces about 2- to 3-inches long. Depending on the purpose, you'll have pieces varying in thickness from $1/8$- to $1/4$-inch thick. Slivers, julienne strips, matchsticks, and French fries are terms used to describe different sizes of shredded ingredients.

Shredding can be done with a knife, cleaver, mandoline, two forks, a shredder or grater, or your hands, provided the food has a definite grain running through it. Meat or poultry should be shredded with the grain. Both should be cut to length first before shredding, to achieve the proper size.

Shaving

The only way to cut paper-thin slices of raw meat or poultry is to shave it. And the easiest way to do that is to partially freeze it first. To shave, you'll need a sharp knife or cleaver and a steady hand.

Chopping

Chopping—this can mean anything from finely minced or diced pieces, to coarsely cut chunks—is best done with a single or double cleaver or chef's knife on a heavy cutting board.

Most cooks prefer wooden chopping boards or blocks (see Utensils & Equipment, page 208). Nowadays, chopping boards are made from numerous materials such as bamboo, plastic, laminate or particle board for food use.

Remember to thoroughly clean or wash off the side of a chopping block used to cut meat (or vice versa) before switching to cut vegetables or fruit to prevent cross-contamination.

Smashing or Crushing

Although these two are not a cutting techniques per se, it is a common technique used in Chinese cooking. Most often used for preparing garlic or ginger, smashing involves placing a piece of food on the chopping board and hitting it with the broad side blade of a cleaver or wide knife. It can be used as is, crushed, or finely minced or chopped.

Processing

When time is at a premium, a food processor can be useful for grinding, chopping, slicing or dicing ingredients such as cabbage, celery, and carrots. It can come in handy to grind meats or seafood for fillings, but be sure to control the processing of the blade to maintain the texture you need.

Cooking Methods & Preconditioning

Each method used in Chinese cooking produces a different result. Some recipes will list a few cooking methods which I call preconditioning. The last final cooking method produces the character of the dish.

If you understand and master the techniques, you can cook Chinese food using any kind of ingredients. Understand the principles and you've got it made.

Preconditioning

Preconditioning is often the necessary first step required in Chinese cooking, whether it be a simple marinade used to preseason meat or an actual cooking process, such as par-boiling or oil-blanching, used to partially cook food.

Marinating

Marinating is used to season an ingredient: to bring out its natural flavor, to tenderize it (usually by adding a liquid), and to change its texture.

Oil-blanching

Oil-blanching is a form of deep-frying, but done at a lower temperature for a shorter time. It helps to separate ingredients as well as form a light crust to seal in the flavor and juices. It also helps shorten the overall cooking time and creates a uniform texture.

Most professional chefs use some form of oil-blanching, but you rarely see it described in cookbooks. I always mention it to my students because I firmly believe you can broaden your Chinese cooking expertise if you know some of the "trade secrets" such as oil blanching.

Unlike deep-frying, which is actually a complete cooking process, oil-blanching is just a quick frying that is always followed by some other cooking method, such as stir-frying or steaming.

When estimating just how much oil to use, I suggest about 2 cups oil for each cup of food to be blanched at one time. Oil used for blanching and deep-frying is reusable. Allow oil to cool. Pour all the oil, except any residue on the bottom, through a fine strainer directly into a jar or bottle fitted with a tight-sealing lid. Refrigerate for up to 1 month.

The oil temperature is usually low during blanching, although 3 different levels are mentioned in our recipes:

Lukewarm (275°-300°) is the most commonly used. Ingredients are cooked evenly and this is a good temperature for preconditioning large quantities.

Low (200°) is nicknamed "hot wok and cold oil" and is used for blanching delicate ingredients such as sole and scallops. Its main purpose is to prevent coloration (browning) and to help maintain the shape of the ingredients.

High (350°) is used to seal in flavor, preserve tenderness, and create a crisp texture or light crunch on the outside.

Oil temperature is determined by the ingredients you plan to blanch as well as the texture you want to achieve. Some recipes suggest that you recheck the oil temperature from time to time, especially when doing large quantities over a long period of time. The easiest way to determine oil temperature is to use a deep-frying or candy thermometer that reads from 200° to 450° attached to the side of the wok.

Water-blanching

Water-blanching, used primarily for vegetables, is a simple process where ingredients are immersed in boiling water for just a few minutes. The vegetables are partially cooked and have been "sealed," locking in vital nutrients and flavor.

I usually recommend blanching in chicken broth, if available, because its rich flavor is absorbed readily, especially by bland-tasting vegetables. Just like oil, chicken broth can be recycled for future use, too. Allow it to cool and then pour through a fine strainer into a jar or bottle. Refrigerate up to 2 weeks or freeze.

Some Chinese recipes combine vegetables. Firmer ones, such as broccoli and carrots, need to be blanched slightly longer than softer ones like snow peas. If you skip water-blanching and simply try to stir-fry 4 or 5 different vegetables, you will find it difficult to be able to cook them evenly in a wok or skillet.

Vegetables that are preconditioned by water-blanching retain their crunchy taste and fresh color, cook more evenly and retain much of their nutrients.

Parboiling

Parboiling is just that—the partial boiling of food. It preconditions tougher cuts of meat and removes impurities. Root vegetables such as potatoes, and other firm ingredients benefit from this method. Quite often, ingredients used in stewing or braising have been parboiled first.

Cooking

Stir-frying

Its name conveys action—keeping the ingredients in constant motion by stirring or tossing with a spoon or wok spatula.

Most stir-fried recipes follow this sequence: preheat the wok, add oil to coat sides to prevent sticking, add spices (or enhancers such as ginger and garlic) and stir until fragrant, add main ingredients while quickly tossing, stir in seasoning sauce, and finally thicken the sauce just before serving.

I like to cook over a fairly high heat because it produces a "wok aroma" or fragrance that is produced from spices added just before the main ingredients. Ginger and green onion and perhaps garlic are good examples. As they begin to heat

Executive Chef Frank Liou shows the sizzle of deep-frying rice noodles. They puff in seconds, yet remain white and delicate.

in a very hot wok, they give off an aroma that signals you to move on to the next step. Practice is the best way to perfect your ability to smell a wok's aroma.

When vegetables are stir-fried, it takes only a few minutes, especially if they have been preconditioned or water-blanched. You want them to be al dente or slightly crunchy when removed from the heat because they continue to cook from the heat they've acquired.

There are some instances where intense heat, almost to the point of smoking, is needed. Vegetables that have lots of water, such as bean sprouts, and other tender ingredients such as liver and squid, require just a few seconds in a hot wok to bring out their flavor. You want to preserve their tenderness and texture by not overcooking.

If you need to, cook in batches. Overloading a wok can cause burning because not enough oil remains in the bottom. Overloading also causes the high heat to dissipate too quickly, so the temperature does not remain high enough, so you have to cook the food longer, resulting in soggy food that steams rather than sizzles or fries.

Deep-frying

Before we get into deep-frying, let me offer an observation about Chinese cooking and the use of oils. Despite the great amount of oil used, Chinese food isn't greasy, or it shouldn't be. Ingredients are cooked very quickly and they don't sit in oil for a long time. The secret is to use the correct oil temperature.

Deep-frying does require more oil than stir-frying. I usually suggest 3 cups of oil for each cup of food. As I mentioned before, maintaining the proper temperature is essential. Unless otherwise noted, 350° to 375° is the normal temperature range for deep-frying.

I've discovered that an electric deep-fat fryer or wok with a reliable thermostat (one that gives you the actual temperature in degrees) can be very helpful. Although I always recommend using a thermometer, at least when beginning Chinese cooking, you can learn to judge the approximate temperature of oil in a wok this way.

Drop a small amount of batter into the oil. If the temperature is:

Under 300°: Batter will drop to the bottom
300°–325°: Batter will drop down and rise slowly
325°–350°: Batter will come up immediately
350°–375°: Batter will not reach the bottom at all
Over 375°: Batter will splatter on the surface

You can deep-fry many different ways, depending on the ingredients used and the texture you want to create.

Dry deep-fry: No batter is used, just dry flour or cornstarch. Deep-fry until the surface reaches a golden brown. Using a higher temperature prevents the flour from separating from the food during frying. Dragon-whiskered Prawns (page 90) is an example.

Soft deep-fry: Marinated ingredients are coated with batter and then deep-fried until golden brown. Sweet & Sour Pork (page 114) is a good example.

Crispy deep-fry: Ingredients are marinated, then steamed (or sometimes hung to dry) before being deep-fried. Many classic duck dishes are prepared this way.

Seasoned deep-fry: The ingredients are seasoned or marinated before being deep-fried. See Chinkiang Pork Chops (page 119).

Double-fry: Either with or without batter, this process is designed for large pieces that often cannot cook completely at one time. First the food is fried at a low temperature, to partially cook it; then the temperature is raised, and it is deep-fried again to create a crisp texture on the outside. Lemon Chicken (page 69) is a good example.

Steaming

Steaming is done over boiling water where steam cooks the food. A dish or ingredients are placed in a rimmed plate or a bowl, then placed on a steamer rack inside a covered steamer or wok.

Steaming cooks food in its own natural juices, helps flavors penetrate all the ingredients, and maintains the food's original shape.

Most dishes can be steamed in a metal steamer or wok fitted with a tight lid and a steamer rack. However, for soft items such as Chinese pastries and buns, it's best to use a bamboo steamer. Because the baskets stack, you can steam several different dishes at once. For an impressive display, bring the steaming basket to the table for serving.

Dry-steaming is a process where food is placed in a bowl, covered, and then set in the steamer. Other recipes require a mold (or bowl). Slices or bite-size pieces of food are decoratively arranged inside the mold; the mold is then placed in the steamer to cook. When ready to serve, invert the mold onto a serving platter.

Braising

In braising, meat, fish or firm vegetables are sometimes browned in a little oil. Then they're cooked in a small amount of liquid over low heat until the liquid is reduced to a sauce and the spices have penetrated the food. A good example of this process can be found in the recipe for Szechuan Dry-braised Prawns (page 94).

Red Cooking

Red cooking, or *hung tsau*, is a Chinese term referring to a slow-cooking process similar to stewing. Meat is browned first and then cooked in plenty of liquid—usually dark soy sauce and other seasonings—until tender. Cooking time ranges from 1 to 4 hours, and the result is a succulent piece of meat with a robust, reddish-brown color.

Associating

Associating means combining assorted ingredients that are precooked and preconditioned. They have either been oil-blanched, deep-fried, or boiled. After combining the ingredients, the dish is cooked for a short time over high heat to bring out the various kinds of flavors.

Pan-frying or Wok-searing

Since a wok can act like a grill, you can pan-fry or brown ingredients with just the slightest amount of oil over a moderate heat. After browning, the food is usually dipped into a sauce or combined with other ingredients.

Poaching

Poaching is "gradual cooking in a liquid over moderate heat." Ginger and green onions add flavor to the poaching liquid.

Smoking

Normally, meat is cured or partially cooked before being slowly smoked. Traditionally, Chinese do their smoke-cooking in a large oven (often outdoors) that contains tea leaves, pine needles, or sawdust from aromatic pieces of wood. During the slow process, the smoky taste permeates the meat. However, a similar smoky taste can be achieved in a shorter time, using a large wok lined with foil. Tea leaves are scattered at the bottom along with a little uncooked rice and sugar. The wok is quickly heated and the smoke penetrates the meat. (See Tea-smoked Duck, page 84.)

Simmering in Master Sauce

A master sauce is a highly regarded soy sauce and spice mixture used to simmer poultry, meat or seafood. It may be used over and over again (see recipe, page 42) if well maintained. Larger pieces of food that have been parboiled or oil-blanched are left to simmer in the master sauce, absorbing all its wonderful flavors.

Cool master sauce before storing airtight in the refrigerator or freezer. Before each use, replenish it by adding more spices and water to return to its original flavor.

Hot Mixing

This cooking term describes combining deep-fried ingredients with a ready-made preheated sauce. You quickly mix the two together and serve. The perfect example of hot mixing is Sweet & Sour Pork (page 114).

Cold Mixing

Most Chinese salads are prepared this way. First, you salt pieces of firm vegetables such as cucumbers or radishes to leach out the excess water and to keep the vegetables crisp. Just before serving, seasonings and a small amount of sesame oil are added.

Baking/Roasting

In China, roasting means something different than it does here. Meat hangs in the middle of an oven instead of being placed on a rack, and the heat source is wood. As the heat circulates evenly around the meat, you're guaranteed a very even kind of cooking. Most restaurants and Chinese grocers or delis roast their ducks or suckling pigs this way. We can accomplish much the same thing in an oven.

Asian Ingredients

These pages provide useful information on many Chinese and Asian ingredients that I use in my cooking. The list is designed to help you understand the ingredients, how to select them, how to prepare them, and how they should be stored. Because the most often asked question in my cooking classes is "What do you recommend?," I have noted my preferences of brand names and sources for ingredients where appropriate.

Agar-agar is a flavorless dried seaweed used like unflavored gelatin. It comes in translucent strands usually sold in strips or sticks, and is used in sweet dishes. Soak agar-agar in warm water for a few minutes to soften before using. Store, tightly wrapped, in a dry location. It lasts almost indefinitely.

Anise (Chinese star) is a star-shape dried seedpod with a flavor similar to licorice. There is no satisfactory substitute for this spice. Sold as whole seedpods, which may be more expensive, and in broken pieces packaged in plastic bags, it can be found in Asian markets, in gourmet shops, or from spice vendors. Store tightly sealed for up to 1 year.

Bamboo Shoots come in cans either sliced, shredded, or whole. They are the edible young fibrous shoots from tropical bamboo. Winter bamboo shoots are dug out of the earth in late winter or very early spring and are more tender than regular bamboo shoots. Store unused bamboo shoots in a jar filled with fresh water and refrigerate. Change water every few days, for up to 1 week.

Basil is a culinary herb that has a strong anise flavor and aromatic fragrance. *Large-leaf Italian* is the basil used in making pesto; it can be substituted for Thai Basil. *Thai Basil (Siam Queen, bai horapa)* has a more intense licorice aroma and flavor. The dark green, slightly narrower leaves have pointed tips and reddish-purple stems. Thai basil holds its flavor and fragrance better than Italian basil in cooked dishes.

Bean Curd (Fresh *Tofu*), also called **Bean Cake**, is made from puréed soybeans mixed with a coagulant, then pressed into blocks weighing ½ to 1 pound each. It is known for its fine texture and bland taste. It is a staple in Asian cuisine because it is high in protein, inexpensive, and very versatile. Fresh bean curd readily absorbs all the delicious flavors of its dish's components. Store unused fresh bean cake in a container filled with water and refrigerate, changing the water daily, for up to 1 week.

Bean Curd (Fermented Red and Yellow) is bean curd that has been fermented in Chinese wine. Available in jars and cans, it has a strong flavor like salted cheese. Although it is usually served as a condiment, it may be used in cooking to flavor meat or vegetables. Stores in its jar almost indefinitely in the refrigerator.

Bean Curd (Pressed *Tofu*) is compressed to a firm texture and has a delicately fragrant aroma. It comes in many flavors, is usually coffee-colored, and comes in 3- to 4-inch by ¼-inch thick squares. Store tightly wrapped in the refrigerator for 2 or 3 days.

Bean Curd Skins are the dried paper-thin skins that form on soy milk when it is heated. They come in packages trimmed to a 6x10-inch rectangles and are used in soup, in vegetable dishes, and as pastry wrappers for sweet desserts. Store, tightly wrapped, in the freezer for up to 6 months.

Bean Paste (Red) is a sweetened paste made from ground red beans and used as a filling for pastries and buns. Available in cans, it can be kept in a sealed jar and refrigerated for many weeks.

Bean Sauce, also called **Brown Bean Sauce**, is a thick condiment with a pungent, very salty taste made from fermented soybeans. It is available in both cans and jars. It keeps almost indefinitely tightly sealed in the refrigerator. (For hot bean sauce, see **Chili Paste**.)

Bean Sprouts come in two varieties: yellow soybean sprouts are topped by a large yellow bean and are usually found only in Asian markets, while the green mung bean sprouts are available in most supermarkets all year round. When selecting sprouts, make sure they are very fresh, crisp and white, with no wilted or brownish tinge present. Store in the refrigerator for 3 to 4 days. Canned bean sprouts are available, but lack the crunchy texture, so I don't recommend them.

Bean Threads (*Mung* Bean Threads; Cellophane, Tranparent, or Glassy Noodles) are translucent, dry, wiry noodles made from *mung* beans. Soak in warm water for 15 minutes before using. Available in small packages, they are used in soup, clay pot and stir-fried dishes. They can be deep-fried in small amounts directly from the package (no soaking) and become instantly puffy and crisp. Store tightly wrapped in a dry location almost indefinitely.

Black Beans (Fermented) are small oval beans preserved in garlic, ginger, and salt. They are primarily used as a seasoning. Sold in packages, they should be rinsed of excess salt, drained, left whole or mashed with other seasonings before using. To store, moisten with oil and place in a tightly sealed jar for up to 1 month or in the refrigerator almost indefinitely.

Black Fungus, Tree Mushrooms or **Cloud Ears** (see **Mushrooms**)

Black Moss or **Black Moss Fungus** (*fat choy*) is a photosynthetic bacteria that grows on the ground in Western China. It is sold dried and needs to be reconstituted briefly before cooking. It has a delicate soft texture, like superfine vermicelli, and is added to dishes at the last minute of cooking. It does not have much flavor, but absorbs the flavor of a dish. In the Chinese New Year greeting *Gung Hay Fat Choy*, using *fat choy* in a dish is symbolic of wishing you good fortune or increased wealth.

Cabbages are varied and plentiful in China and Asia but are increasing available here.

Bok choy has a long, smooth white stem and large, dark green chard-like leaves. Its flavor is delicate and is used in stir-frying and in soups. *Shanghai baby bok choy* or *bok choy hearts* are smaller versions of this family. *Napa* or *Chinese cabbage* has a tightly packed head of broad white or ivory stems fringed with yellow to pale green leaves folded over the top and has a fresh taste when lightly cooked. *Chinese broccoli* (*gai lan*) have deep green stalks with sparse green leaves, small flower buds and a slightly bitter taste—excellent in stir-fried dishes or when water-blanched.

Cardamom is a small, aromatic pod-shaped fruit with seeds inside. Sold packaged either as whole pods, seeds, or ground, it is used as a scasoning in Master Sauces or as a spice. Store in a tightly sealed jar for up to 1 year.

Caul Fat is the fatty tissue, resembling lace or netting, that comes from the inner organs of pigs. It is used to wrap food during cooking to retain shape and flavor. It is available from good butchers, or ordered in advance. Store unused portion, tightly wrapped, in the freezer for up to 4 months.

Chili Flakes are the crushed seeds and skin of dried hot chili peppers. This is not the same as chili powder, which is a mixture of many different spices.

Chili Oil is a combination of red chili peppers cooked in oil. It is easy to make your own, although it is readily available bottled in Asian markets and some super-markets. Store airtight for up to 1 year.

Chili Paste is a mixture of ground fresh or dried chilies with other ingredients such as garlic, spices, vinegar, lime juice, beans and vegetable oil. Also called **Hot Chili Bean Sauce** (*sambal oelek*) it is used as a spicy condiment or seasoning in Asian dishes. Store, tightly sealed, in the refrigerator for 3 to 4 months.

Chili Pods are just that; dried, whole red chili pods. If crushed, they are called chili flakes. Store, tightly wrapped, in a dry location almost indefinitely.

Chinese Barbecue Sauce (see *Sa Cha* **Sauce**)

Chinese Blanched Chives or **Yellow Chives** are also called garlic chives, which resemble green onions and are available with green or blanched yellow leaves (grown without sunlight). Both look like scallions, but the leaves are flat. The flavor ranges between garlic, leek and onion. Yellow chives are milder in flavor than the green, and are used in delicate dishes that require a subtler flavor and color. Store in a plastic bag for 3 to 4 days in the refrigerator.

Chinese Broccoli (*gai lan*) is a vegetable used more for its stalk and leaves than for its flower, as with Western broccoli. Its deep green stalks and leaves have a mild, slightly bitter taste. It is used blanched or in stir-fries and is best cooked crisp-tender. It is often served blanched with a drizzle of oyster sauce. It is very nutritious. Store in a plastic bag in the refrigerator for up to 5 days.

Chinese Parsley, also known as **Cilantro** or **Coriander**, is a flat-leafed herb that

Celebration Menus

When preparing a special Chinese dinner menu, plan for contrasts: from spicy to mild, crunchy to tender, smooth, sweet and salty. A variety of tastes and textures make each course an adventure. Vary the ingredients and flavors so the dishes complement one another— follow a seafood course with a meat, poultry or vegetable dish, and end with a scrumptious and unexpected dessert. Most importantly, plan a menu around the special dishes you enjoy eating and preparing. The menus here are just a starting point—substitute another dish or limit the entrées depending on how many people you are going to serve and what dishes you think they might enjoy.

p65

MENU I

In Your Honor: A Special Birthday Dinner

p32

Appetizer
Grilled Honey-glazed Quail With Watercress Salad

Soup
Ginger Clam

p107

Wok-seared Rack of Lamb With Lemon Grass

p139

Dungeness Crab With Golden Garlic Crust

Gung Gung's Home-style Oxtail Stew
Served With Long-Life Noodles

p132

p180

Dessert
Sesame Taro Rolls

p27

MENU II

A Reason to Celebrate!

p60

Appetizer
Minced Crystal Prawns With Toasted Pine Nuts

Soup
Kabocha Bisque

p128

Orange Blossom Ribs

Maine Lobster Yee-mein

Fresh Basil Beef

Miso-crusted Sea Bass

p135

Taiwan Aboriginal Sticky Rice

p108

Dessert
Pineapple Crescents

p164

p99

p188

215